Leakage & Smoke

Richard Martin

ARTWORK
t thilleman

SPUYTEN DUYVIL
New York City

Acknowledgements

Some of these poems have appeared in the following publications. Thanks to the editors of: *Abbey, Aurora, Big Hammer, Chiron Review, Estuaires* (Luxembourg) *Gargoyle, Fell Swoop: The All Bohemian Revue, Hurricane Review, Lummox, Sky Island Journal* and *OZ BURP* (Australia)

Pastoral, Landing, Time of Togetherness and *Brilliant Skies of Stars* first appeared in the mini-chapbook, *Landing* (Moron Channel Publications). My thanks to editor and publisher, XJ Dailey.

Library of Congress Cataloging-in-Publication Data

Names: Martin, Richard, 1949- author.
Title: Leakage & smoke / Richard Martin.
Other titles: Leakage and smoke
Description: New York : Spuyten Duyvil, [2023]
Identifiers: LCCN 2023012929 | ISBN 9781959556282 (paperback)
Subjects: LCGFT: Poetry.
Classification: LCC PS3563.A7277 L43 2023 | DDC 811/.54--dc23/eng/20230327
LC record available at https://lccn.loc.gov/2023012929

LEAKAGE & SMOKE

CONTENTS

VIGILANCE

I am given wings for a purpose.
Cloud formations have been too dark lately;
the sky rarely shimmers.
"Polish them," my boss says,
"and don't screw up."

Years ago, I worked as a carhop at A & W.
Employees were required to wear roller skates.
It was about efficiency, getting the burgers and fries
to the cars as fast as one could skate.
My co-worker was an Elvis impersonator.
He smacked me in the head and said:
"I serve the pretty girls, not you."

I've never been to China and can't read or speak Chinese.
The poem, "China" by Bob Perelman, is a favorite of mine.
As an aerialist, I like the line:
Even the words floating in the air make blue shadows.
But I know the owner of a Chinese restaurant swore at me
in Chinese for being an incompetent dishwasher.

These are the abbreviations of clouds under my purview:
(Ci) (Cc) (Cs) (Ac) (As) (Ns) (Cu) (Cb) (Sc) (St).
As for shades of blue, I prefer cerulean.

On occasion, hunters mistake me for a duck
and empty both barrels.
Drones buzz me on a regular basis.
Escape from reality remains a passion of mine.
Remember when everyone went cosmic,
wore flowers in their hair? Said: "Peace."
Love was on the loose.

I don't work when it rains.
Off days, I sit in my yard in an Adirondack chair,
a shotgun on my lap.
There are reports of robots delivering packages
in the neighborhood.
I am ready for them, vigilant and wet.

Sex on the Beach

The purpose of the title
Is to define
The temporal geography

We know each other
Agree the demise of literacy
Elects disingenuous candidates

There are problems associated
With drinking alone
Memory suspects interior motives

Media tinkers with emotions
Mistakes rebound
Meaning succumbs to geriatric light

Histrionic obfuscation shrouds
The value of a timely kiss
During high tide

ALIEN DNA

Just when
I tipped my hat
to greet the wind,
I noticed something
I had never seen before.
I was quite sure, positive
to be exact, that it wasn't a
flower, some exotic type, or
a small unknown fish, pepper
in color with green eyes, or an
unexplored mountain range, or
even a foreign desert landscape,
things that I had actually seen and
discussed with friends and neighbors.
This was raspberry-tinted in color with
eyes of granite, short and stout in stature,
possessed of a large blue tongue, which at
at regular intervals it stuck out at individuals
passing by in hurried oblivion. The tongue un-
dulated like an ocean wave whipped into a wild
frenzy by a barbarous wind. No one saw or paid
the slightest attention to the words emblazoned on
on the tongue: *hopeless*, *deluded*, *stupid*, words, by
Executive Order, banned from our national vocabulary.
A hefty fine was imposed on any citizen who used any-
one of them to describe a political leader, specifically the
US president. The raspberry-tinted visitor began to hop up
and down and all around in expanding circles as my faithful
and tardy bus arrived. I entertained the possibility that I might
be home in bed or even, god forbid, hallucinating when I paid
my fare and found my seat. Timid at first, but then with convic-
tion, I looked out the window to wave goodbye to the raspberry-
tinted visitor and resume a more rational outlook on the nature of

things,
but "poof"
it was gone.

Love Letters

I'm a proponent of the art of sending letters
in the form of a poem to those who prefer
not to read letters or poems, let alone
a letter in the form of a poem.

It used to be quite the rage.

Dear Frank,

      The wild stallion in my backyard wrecked the barbeque
after refusing to do party tricks for the guests. My wife left me
for a metaphor with a boss set of wheels and impressive pecs.
The marriage is done.
      I can't watch the news on tv anymore. To me, it is a
form of sickness and conveys humans in the final stage
of their regrets. I speaking dinosaurs here, my friend, but
don't quote me on it.
      I still enjoy sunsets and their fiery displays, and the
purple lips pursuing me in last night's dream were enticing
enough for me to kiss my pillow.
      I'm not lonely. But I've collected too much
road dust and it's weighing me down.
      I hope your refrigerator is adequately filled with beer.
      Mine isn't.

Yours,
Harry

PS   There's a guy on my street who took a shot at a well-known poet at one of the
well-known universities in the city. He substituted potato salad and lemon
meringue pie for buckshot. Remember how potato salad was weaponized in
Howl? I avoid eye-contact with him when we pass each other on the street.

Pastoral

The pen creates the necessary ecstasies. We meet in a meadow of gems.

Words produce frondescent trees. My mind needs a break.

"Turn to the sky for information," you say.

Birds arrive in green feathers of dawn. When it is time for lunch

we abandon time & order what has been lost during former lives.

"Make sense of the world," the waiter says.

"Coherence please," pleads the bus exhaust.

All around us are the tall windows of others' wonder. Some are having their

blood pressures checked. Some forge checks to buy unlisted countries on the market.

The ability to reside in carnal and dissonant sentences restores mellifluent hesitations in

prized associations.

"Thou art perception," a roadhouse saint proclaims from the pulpit of a chrome

hog, rutting in traffic.

Jewels of stress flash through clouds. Precocious leaves marry the ground.

"Holy," you say, without pretending somehow.

Why I'm Not an Intellectual

Who pays any attention to a guy like me

Migratory birds rest in my hair

I smoke unfiltered cigarettes in nonsmoking environments

The English Oxford Dictionary broke three of my toes

I still use pickup lines

Idiots adore me

Animals think I'm one of them

I like to argue with inanimate objects

Drugs did something to my brain

I flunked Philosophy 101

Literary criticism pisses me off

I was dropped on my head at birth

There are too many eggheads already

I chase the past down the street to the horror of neighbors

Spacetime is two words not one

I abhor evaluation and interpretation

Mensa has a Restraining order on me

I never vacate the premises

I memorize what I forget

My brain is a scrambled egg

I don't use punctuation

REQUIRED TEXT

1

I wrapped this poem
In a wealth of cosmic lines.
Step on/Step off the boatman ordered
The unqualified passengers.
O the blue wings of dawn caught us by surprise!
Again, the hermeneutic raised its ugly head,
Arguing vociferously with the ledger of space
Right into the guts of time.
If you've been listening to the home orchestra,
A round of holidays pledged support
For the vacuous candidate.

2

There was some hesitation during the matinee
Of the perplexed.
Deep in the recesses of the brain
The reason for death encountered a problem.
O small words crept into a dark corner!
That's when smartphones were confiscated
By a teenage billionaire with attitude.
Gag order in place,
The verbose entrepreneur huffed and puffed.
Seated at a table of pathological liars,
She passed the caviar without incident.

3

In an act of brazen pillows,
You revolted with the rest of the sunflowers.
I headed down a verdant highway
In hot pursuit of the Theory of Everything.
O sunset arrived in indigo pasties!
They wanted a new language,
One devoid of reference and incorrigible syntax.
Leave the rose alone,
Members of the string quartet ordered.
It was raining a thicket of minutes
In a world still visible and there.

Hoax Bubble

Here's what these words mean.
You're riding a horse into a Montana sunset.
Bleached bones entangled with meandering stars.
A call for order in a coyote's eyes.
Brick mountains and insufferable equations.

You could whistle a tune by Mozart.
Join the cause.
Enough dead in Afghanistan.
Media speak and lost mothers harmonize.
Language is a tattletale.

Now for the sands of incomprehension.
At the Alphabet Hotel, a botched press conference.
Sacred routes double-crossed toxic chemicals.
Europeans consider Americans stupid.
Babble in the neocortex.

My Lover Says

It's time for words
to flash erotic instructions
I live in a banana Republic

Want to Bees   Want to Bees

Saffron clouds paint the sky
when she steps from her negligee
Is the news recycled in a bubblegum machine

My lover says
which hat

Which words would you choose to flash
Why not commit to angels in a tree of birds
Take a number is a powerful command

Want to Bees   Want to Bees

The resident expert testifies on Court TV
life's side effects proliferate into side effects
I water the flowers inside of me

Want to Bees   Want to Bees

My lover says
this hat

Reflection on reflection
reflects too much reflection
Neurons are quantum highways

Want to Bees   Want to Bees

The man who stole my ski hat camps
on an iceberg in *National Geographic*
Did the world just grunt or was that the can opener

My lover says
time to go

AFTERNOON NAP

Life unbuttoned death.
I saw you in the clouds is what you said.
I rode my bicycle in a hail of red rubber balls.
Daffodils whipped by wind into yellow flags,
Before silence spread it wings and rose into the air.

I wrote today's date on a small rock
And left for England.
There were so many seagulls in my line of sight,
I had another drink – bottle of Chardonnay with twisted cap.
Some passengers wore masks; some fought in the aisle.

When the queen refused to see me, I landed
On a park bench in Dublin by the river Liffey,
Conversed with the ghost of James Joyce.
It seemed amused by my exhaustion.
Why I waded into memories for lost treasure.

The sky pawned diamond trinkets for emptiness.
I discovered the small rock in my pocket on the way home.
It moved in my hand like a family of waves.
Fish recited the calendar of days.
Time seemed unimportant.

POSTCARDS

1

Hair a mess.
Suffering a terrible sunburn.
Latest work panned by critics.
Keel-billed toucan watches my every step.
Al Capone played his banjo in jail.

2

Umbrella a kite.
Words fly from mind into a pocket dictionary.
What does musophobist mean?
Are you one?
Wind ululates.

A Select Group of Renegades

The book washed ashore in a deluxe

        edition of yesterday.

It started in high school and blossomed

        in the space between ideologies.

Some wanted a wall – others a redefinition

        of matter and its hegemonic invisibility.

Then a virtual spaceship

        touched down in the O.K. Corral.

Characters in the text ordered a cherry soda

        polished their silver pistols.

Time lost direction.

Was it time to eat a peach?

There were equations to balance in the soft-spoken Academy of Now.

Simultaneity became a popular name for newborns.

A select group of renegades conferred on a private beach.

Thunder arose in the body politic.

CONFESSION

I'm guilty
Blue jays bicker in hemlocks
Autumnal sun warms my feet

I am reading
A light breeze kisses my cheek
All property is theft

Pierre-Joseph Proudhon
There's a swing set with a red slide
Japanese maple in the yard

Breeze picks up
I'm sailing
Ghost planes in the sky

What the hell did I do
Each day we're told
The world's not healthy

Eventually the mind goes sick
We play lopsided games
In spacetime

Think visions
Will carry us beyond
The limits of matter

Rocks in the yard are beautiful
Because I want them to be granite
they are

Codes for immanence & transcendence
Colonize thought   Sometimes
The squeeze of happiness hurts

Everything is holy
On a pale green table
A green beetle basks in the sun

The wand of osculation
Loose in the shed
Door open

Fat Ankles

I went back to the language
Of what I knew about the world
With a laundry list of things
To consider

Abridged

1. Blackbirds in the yard
2. A woman on the street in shades
3. A white dog on a leash beside her
4. Blossoms of rhododendron
5. Sunlight
6. Write the mayor

I wrote the mayor (excerpt below)

"What has happened to all the snow?"
"Where is the wind that whistled through the branches of my bones?"
"Explain the single leaf of consciousness waving like a retired flag?"

No response (reaction below)

I got hot under the collar
Shed my clothes
Turned on the tv

Swarms of politicians told me I'd have more money in my pocket
Under their guidance "Fuck the rest of the world," one of them said,
Prancing around the stage like a show horse

Thank God THE MEDIA explained what it all meant
"Show horse" was a euphemism for mindless politicians
"No one running for office (with or sans head) should use swear words when
addressing potential voters," a pundit on a panel of them counseled, "because voters
never use swear words when communicating with each other and an inappropriate

use of language could increase the collective blood pressure of the country or possibly
cause those in bars to buy a round of drinks
for their friends."

My intention was to reset the linearity of my mind to spin cycle
Form a hypothesis on the paradise embedded in every moment
Do something about my fat ankles

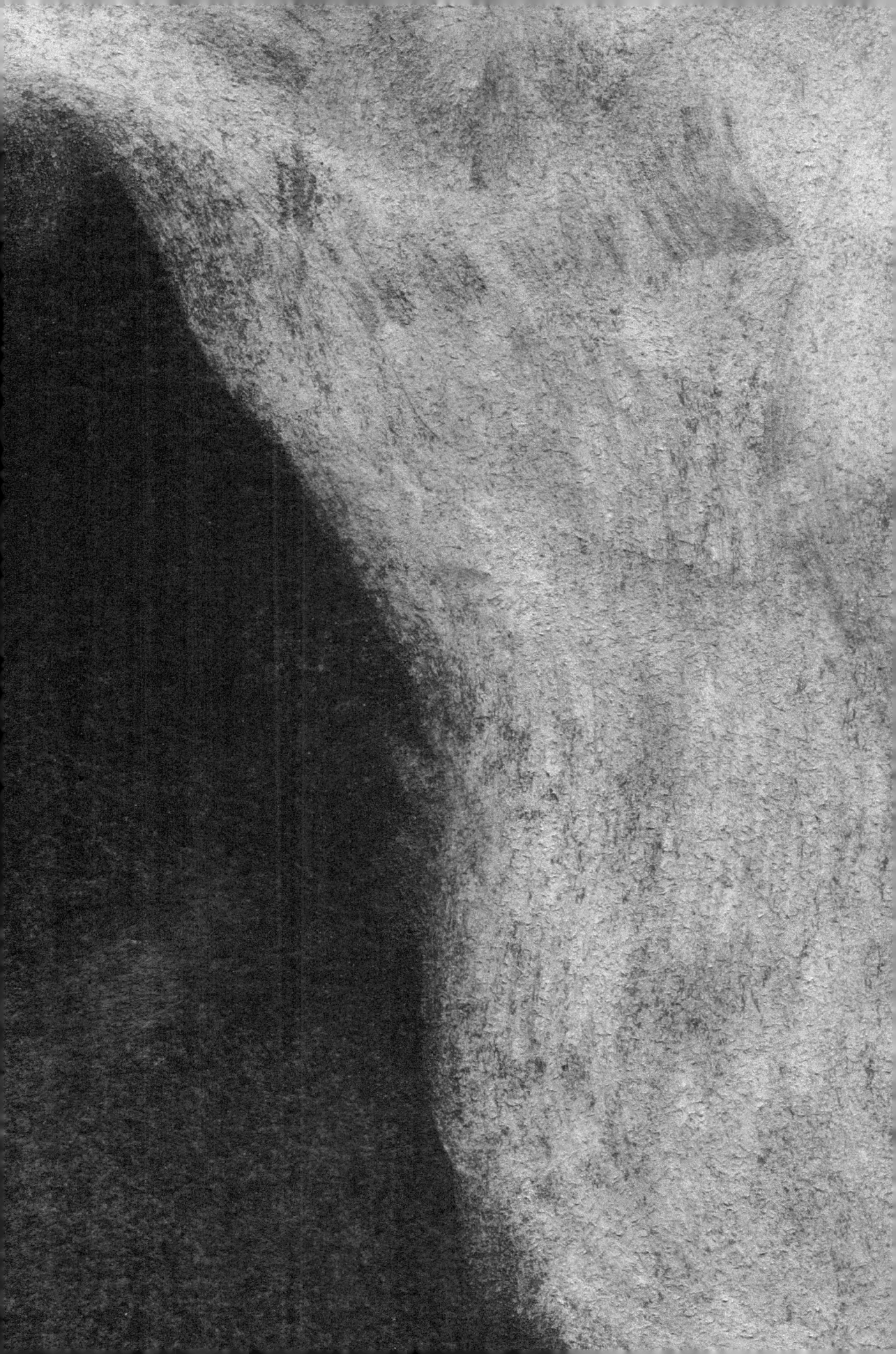

Reverie on a New Pillow Case

Just breathing
Sky without sun
The hieroglyphics of yesterday –
Pollen in hyphenated wind
You and I live in our brains now
We're not kids anymore
Language fans colorful...forgets
Hesitates   A motif peacock
It waits for us to find
Something to say

Picking up where thought left off
Young and one
Swinging in the yard under historic maples
Imagination blues: bright eyes and plenty
Of speed in the veins
Running headlong into song
Open expanses of sunlight
Ample list of no concerns
Learning to play the ukulele
Telling on time

Come to the table of plain speech
One more circular to read
Another in the mail by a sad hand
Overhead satellites snap
Classified photographs
Is that you with the all-day lollipop
And devious eye   or me
Putting on socks after a day at the beach
Surge ocean is our only hope
Smile former lives

HERE

"Sky" is a word.
Today, rain.
Tomorrow, a bowtie of sunset,
as earth slips into a virtual trance.
Goes missing.
Oceans die in a lap dance of excuses.
Who said: "Nature's party is trampled by our footprints?"
Wordsmiths of destruction. Maybe. Fill in the
_____with a nanosecond narrative.
Meanwhile, polar bears float on ice blocks across continents;
world leaders check their bank accounts before sleep.
Everyone with a pocket dictionary proceeds
to the next destination.
In the long haul of signs,
where are we?

BOLT MISSING

The rhythm of the dance is sky.
Sentences resist make-up on mayhem.
Sleep Sleep now in the dream of now.
Right now. Over here. Next to...
Bird imitations, the mystery of song.
Tree sweetly in the sweet morning. Not
Yet. Refreshed we are.
The rain of memory over.
The reign of what?

O cans of consciousness, you say.
Market raw and fluctuating
Minus feathers, pillows of persuasion.
Pitter patter of little feats in the capital dawn.
What's that?
The rhetorical mystery of a missing hat?
Love machine on empty.
Emancipated night in long johns. Silver.
Panning for it in the brainpan.

A screw loose in the syllable pie.
We know that in the post post post of post.
Raven mask. Talk radio.
Beat of drums in the appetite jungle.
Unshakeable hands whiteout mistakes.
Evolved tongue in the wounds of night.
Listen, we're listening.
Waves of feet. Waves of everything.
Water tight.

DAILY GRIND

Textual hopes/textual dopes   by way of ear
language inspires the mind   provokes the conscious stream

I'm here today as a fish before the advent of designer bombs
Emissary to what I don't understand

I left my pet avatar on a dark chandelier
Does syntax corroborate existence

I think therefore I'm thought   fruit fly in still life
blackbird in the dead of night ... (Free Plagiarism Checker)

Word is out   womb of stars is our petri dish

Recent scholarship on Jesus asserts he never claimed
to be divine   Love is   I know what it means to kiss
you in raging surf   to pursue a salty text

We're long shots my old man used to say   before
landing a good one on my arm

STRUMMING

I know the world is out there.
I hear it banging on the windows and jumping on the roof.
It wants access to my room, to come in and sit for a while,
school me on its recent history or past, maybe
explore the latest idea in the mind of a lonely physicist.
Why not? Ideas ricochet off neurons during coffee breaks,
while skiing down an Alpine slope – the nothingness
of an idea itself in the full attire of a boating accident on Lake Samsara.
But who knows what the world wants when in a tantrum on windows and roof?
I could try to serenade it with my guitar,
as if it were a lover in a red party dress on moonlit balcony.
This banging and jumping are spoiling my nerves.
I'm pretty sure history lessons and nothingness are bogus.
But there is no way for me to play innocent bystander, just
another human in for the night.
The world is incessant, an unappeasable ancient child.
"Hey knucklehead!" it shouts at me. "Wake up!"
Jesus, this was supposed to be a night of solitude for me,
one without the latest news or the inconsolable world
outside my windows and on my roof.
I've chosen a good book and steam rises from my teacup.
I have no use for the apocalyptic tenor of the times,
intrusion into my safe house.
The world is distraught.
I know plenty of songs where love
forms notes ascending into the sky.
I start to play.

Winter through a Gray Window

I was dizzy and searched for a cause.
Maybe the spin of the earth caught me napping in my chair.
I could have been cast into deep space with an outdated star map.
Orion appeared and slipped into a deck of cards. Why?

I used to be a ballroom dancer,
wined and dined in a cloudburst of inopportune moments,
until the sun heated the spare change in my pockets.
No regret in trees stalking me on my perilous way.

Coherence started to plague me.
Words slipped on slopes of mind.
We were on our way to create the perfect society.
Everyone knew hate sucked.

Love was free – dominion of souls,
minus the history of previous encounters with Eros.
A oneness felt in the marrow of bones –
the spontaneous kiss in the glaring headlights of night.

Everything started again at the beginning.
First Cause paced back and forth on a velvet carpet of nothingness.
Reasons and questions clumped into galaxies without ultimate answers.
It was hard to avoid dizziness after standing up too fast.

THAT'S THAT

OK   tiger
sprinkle the air with silence

Let   Buddha wait
think
fast
tell jokes in the poolhall

feel the nerves
in his nervous heart

*

History is a stitch in my side
It's tough to elude a nightmare of clouds

Extension of syllables into space
is a formal suggestion

O the conversation behind curtains
leaps like a cat

*

The pain of the immediate hides
in the laundromat

Enjoy nostalgia while you can

Realism washes to shore
in plastic bottles

*

The icon's eyeballs reflect insane politicians
I wore a sportscoat in high school

What we forget never makes up
for the times we stood in line
for tickets

*

Desire for the unknown feeds the soul
Mind projects a shapely beauty

Objects entertain consciousness
Creation is a jocular enterprise

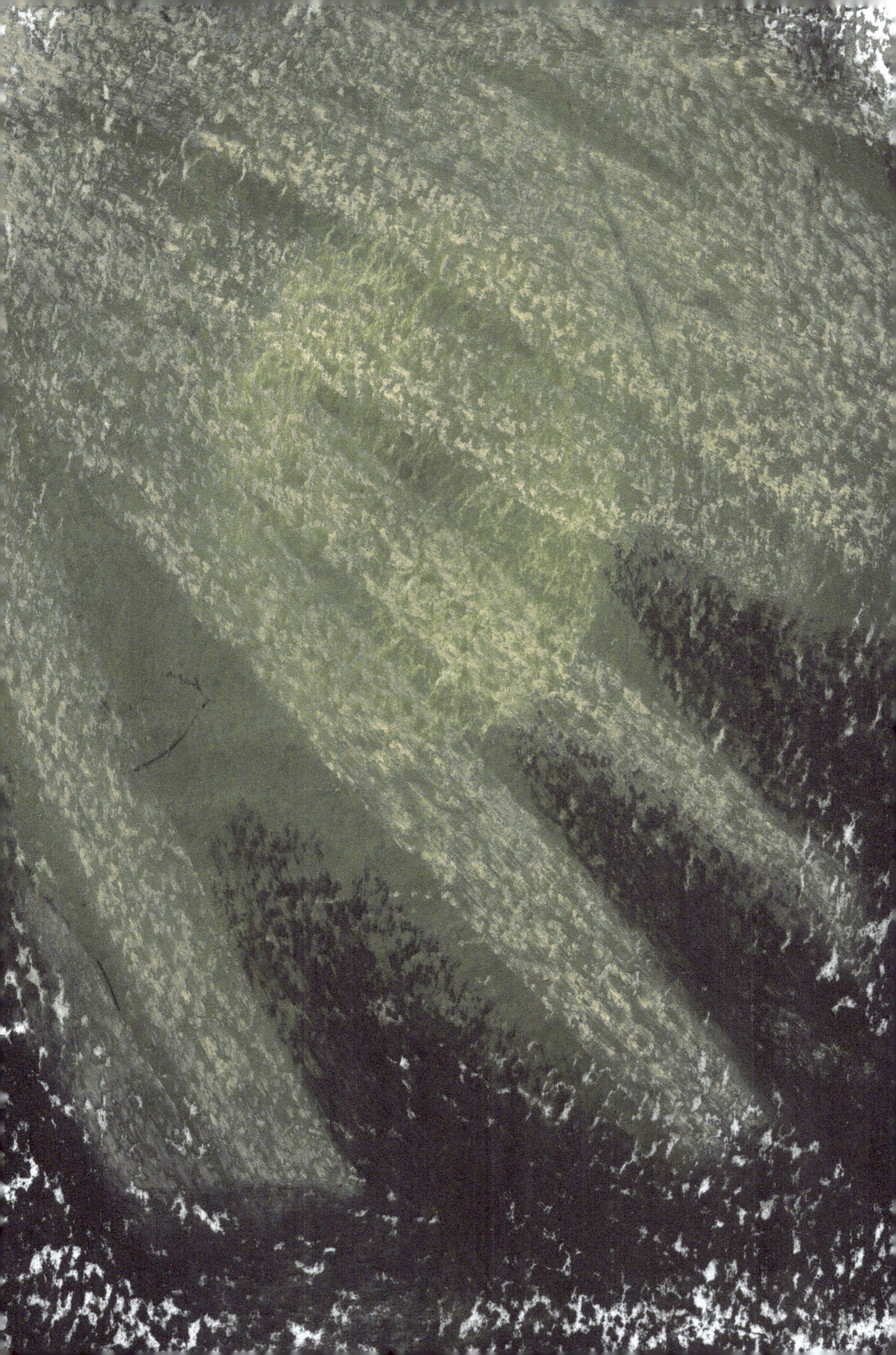

ACCEPTANCE OF CLOWNS

The news competes with entertainment
A balloon rises above a field of hostile grasshoppers
A red-carpet pontiff faints
The sun rises as an immaculate being
There is an accident
Police chase
A bombshell at the wheel

A jazz of chemical explosions
Commercials for drugs to relieve bloating
The invention of IQ
Entropy vs foreclosure
A castle vs superhighway through the yard
A suitcase of lost airports
Is how the solar system views it

The fun of cooking for one
The wild ride on a flattening molecular cloud
Why your mother-in-law visits or not
We could love each other without religion
Stop shooting each other because of it
No one is too plain
Accept blame

Let's not melt the rest of the polar ice caps
Remember to give coherence the cold shoulder
I've just been rejected by an online magazine
Divorced in Vegas
Tell the pathological truth
What's up with you
Got Red Nose

Time Travel

for JCW

The day she stretched across my body,
I didn't realize time had different plans for us.
Now a faucet leaks and kids in the neighborhood
have disappeared into screens.
They bet the only parallel universe is digital.
Before parting, we smoked Marlboros.

In 1948, anyone could buy a Cuban cigar
after a hot turkey sandwich at the Astor Place Luncheonette.
Rudy Burckhardt's *Astor Place, 1948* photo confirms that.
You could also purchase a tie at the Astor Neckwear Shop,
enjoy a billboard of Coca Cola with an Amazon daughter
of Ares and Harmonia.

This morning I vanished in a forest of sunflowers.
My neighbor grows them and they loom above the sidewalk
as puppets of sunshine. He offers them as a refuge
for those who chose to disappear into light. No charge!
I've considered the value of a facial to change
the calculus of things, too.

My wife thinks I'm dissatisfied – reason for my odd behavior.
John Stith Pemberton invented Coca Cola in the late 19th century.
It's two main ingredients were coca leaves and kola nuts.
It was concocted as patient medicine, a stimulating
temperance drink for those who could use one.
I could go for the original recipe now.

Lost Dogs

It's not a great situation
too many
rising from the dead
with plans
of their own.
Some claim a claustrophobic
reaction
to eternity. Others complain
about the size of park benches
inside stars.
So, they're here,
smashing street lights
and mocking
the living space assigned
to memories
that tag
after us
like lost dogs.

Conspiracy of Orbit

What orbits me comes in capsules of owl & forgetfulness. I used to play the
saxophone on laundry days, wore socks that matched conflicting opinions on the
afterlife. I searched for form in all the wrong places. As I remember, the porcelain
forest, next to the portrait of abandoned ideas in the living room, caused the interruption
in the latest news cycle.

Duck-n-cover drills were passé. Active shooter drills were in vogue. Please,
don't scare the children with oceans absent of fish, opioid masses, plus the paraphernalia
of so much more.

At some point, I purchased a smartphone. Everyone was online. No one followed
Jesus anymore. Even on Twitter! The government could locate me; hackers stole and sold
my anonymity.

"Get with it," I pleaded with myself.

I appeared on C-SPAN – mimicked silence and restraint during an inundation
of Robocalls from candidates on steroid ideologies. Agents of change offered a tax break
of threats and exile.

Vote Yes if you believe in No!

Vote No if you believe in Yes!

The planet understands the monetary value placed on it is a temporary setback.

Pathetic Love Poem

I'm so far away from touching you
I could be in the next room,
on a planet shaken from its orbit,
careening freely in space.

It's a numbers game
of walls and darkness, isn't it?
As if you could respond to that question,
find a drill or telescope to see

where I might be, hiding perhaps
in a revision of the past,
imprisoned by a dialogue with the moon
on the nature of romance.

This afternoon I purchased an avenue of birds
and stoked old flowerpots to life
with magic inherited from rain.
My mind works this way;

it sends messages throughout my body,
surreal ones, really,
open to ridicule and false accusations
as if nature took its cue from Lazarus

and unqualified hope.
Once I was covered with tattoos of sunlight
because you kissed my lips
with vigor, hired musicians

for the absence of garments.
We entered nakedness like we knew
what we were doing – sommeliers of flesh.
Your beauty broke the clock on the bed stand

into a single moment.
"Work with that," you said,
as if I could grasp eternity
in the sweat of bodies.

If love had a brain, things would be different.
It would appreciate the way life and death
lie side by side in embryo,
aware of the odds.

MAGNIFICENT MATTER

The text of consciousness
Alters weather and prayers

Words roam with animals
In the valley of truth

The sky flies into focus
Without the alphabet of names

Wine casks perform miracles
For the omnipresent camera

The creative link between time and space
Is no longer the issue

Molecules relinquish their rights
In formless seas

Life steadies itself
on a bad case of nerves

The mind opens for a going
out of business sale

Reincarnation clamors
for recognition

The fix is on
Daylight beckons

Up Ahead

As I predicted, my feet caught fire in a snowstorm.
After that, I was offered money to foretell events.
Simple things: weather without scanning the sky,
middle names of future lovers, how'd folks feel in 20 years.
Their investments channeled unexpected rainbows
in their bedrooms after making love.
"Henry" and "Audrey" struck them as reasonable middle names.
Absence of time in stressed brains two decades hence suited most.

Prophecy proved to be lucrative. I moved into a 5-bedroom house
with a swimming pool and tennis court.
With excess capital, I built a crystal ball factory,
opened crystal ball stores across the country.
The "balls" became a must have item.
People began to predict events in their own lives – the year
they'd go bald, hear a politician tell the truth, win the lottery,
see the earth as their endangered mother.

Smartphones were passé. Everyone walked the streets
with a crystal ball in their hands, had fun gazing into them
waiting for traffic lights to change, a date to appear out of thin air.
There was an uptick in people knowing where they were
or going next. Hostilities between them waned
into a whimper of small complaints.

Things got predictably better. I accepted a sweet time slot
for my own television program, gambling on further success.
I insisted on no script, no commercials, no guests or tricks,
just the show's title: *Up Ahead*.
Millions tuned in. I sat in a chair for 30 minutes
gazing into my crystal ball.
Periodically, I looked up from it, stared into the camera,
and said: "What's next, people?"

Nano-Sermons

*

Mirrors in a swan of shadows reflect transcendence
Horizontal dreams perpetuate opinion polls
O snail of sentences which way goes thy narrative

*

Blue monkeys trouble aesthetics
Imaginary gazelles pillage loaves of bread
Logicians fire pistols into the air and weep

*

Nothing mars omnipresence
Spontaneity promotes gale force winds
Arbitrary selves congeal and explode

*

The all-star bowling team chugs ritual beers
Uber lovers munch on buttered popcorn voraciously
The black sheep in the family bursts into snowflakes

*

Everything shakes to be new in the cataclysm of time
The algebra of the situation requires constant surveillance
Space shatters into subplots

*

Cats piss in flowerpots
Hawks float above canyons
Dragonflies mate over lily pads

*

Internet posts clutter the minds of commuters
It is the age of ubiquitous and duplicitous cameras
Memories compliment the failed infrastructure of time

*

Security cameras spy on rambunctious water bottles
Vagrant symbols mask prying eyes
Apoplexy stokes prediction

*

Raindrops strike seared lips and heartbeats
Beauty persists in the language of shadows
Bodies worship love

*

Screens go blank
Unity requires an unfettered imagination
Reflection is the gig

Menace of Unreality

I walked on the sea of a million nights before

Plants and animals fell from the sky in baskets of extinction

Paraphernalia tossed high by waves entered the mouths of blue whales

Everyone in the watery foam spoke in tongues

All claimed the journey had just begun

The world turned into a dangerous one in the furtive eyes of birds

There was an absence of books on a shelf of clouds

I tried to sleep and dream of *rosy-fingered dawn*

Light filtered the words of the only madman in town

Mystics crossed abandoned streets without paying attention to the flow of traffic

On designated corners concession stands offered insurance on bridal gowns

Flash mobs formed in the alleys of chilled conversations

I went out for pancakes and eggs

Poets were paid huge sums to shut up

Black doors thundered in the morning rain

Those in crystal robes pandered for truth in courtrooms of the robbed

Many flogged their blogs or posted unkempt animals on the loose

A glum planet sought a new orbit

Walking the Dog

Thought is cagey
The mind responds, leaps
Into a sky of bare branches
Bathed in light
The body walks its faithful dog
Cold toes of being absorb
sidewalks, their histories
Cracks and sparkles
It is the winter solstice
So, what is new?
Anthropocene anti-humanists plead
For the end of humanity
Too much destruction of nature
Transhumanists upload the neurons
Of a bat's brain into a laptop computer
Is this a lie or the future?
Immortality lurks somewhere
In technological tricks
The dog observes passing cars,
Stops to sniff a tree trunk,
Dead leaves haloing it
Umwelt
The goal is to lose the self
To use the space to welcome
A void of stars and galaxies
Who made you?
God made you
The imagination plays
In a sandbox of concepts and ideas
Wars continue
Why?
Pumpkins chewed by squirrels
Entertain ponds of frozen water
Light shrinks into what
It has to offer

Knowledge succumbs
To the unknown
Or does it?
The mind takes it in
From the limb
Of a homeless oak
A family forest of them
Gone in the neighborhood
Was the mind once
The soul of a dinosaur
They morphed into birds
Didn't they?
Are mind and soul
interchangeable?
If not, why not?
What about consciousness,
The rivers and tributaries
Of its demeanor?
Could quantum equations
Solve this?
Why did God make you?
To be happy with Him in heaven
The body returns home
Dog rolls back and forth
On the frozen lawn,
Kicking legs
In a spasm of joy
Body gives it a go
Mind wings
Above a sloop
Of clouds

Daydream Cover Charge

Press "here" for entrance into my daydream.

The color of the day is purple haze.

A lunch pail is highly recommended for a sojourn

      through the obstacles of tomorrow.

Smartphones are a necessity and highly recommended.

Consider Scam Likely a friend.

All calls will be monitored until someone smashes my smartphone.

Tik Tok will feature the Mouseketeers Parade in ad infinitum loop.

Walt Disney and Annette Funicello were personal friends of mine.

M I C   KEY   M O U S E.

Avengers will be available throughout the daydream for selfies.

Coffee mugs with the expression: WORLD'S GREATEST LOAFER

      on sale throughout the daydream.

Expect the following literary interruption:

("I loafe and invite my soul, / I lean and loafe at my ease …. observing a spear of summer grass.")

In 2009, The Walt Disney Company acquired Marvel Entertainment for US$4 billion; it has been a limited liability company (LLC) since then.

Thank you, Walt. (*Leaves of Grass*, Walt)

I did pirate info about The Walt Disney Company from the Internet.

Peugeot was the first LLC on the planet.

Suggested reading: Harari's *Sapiens A Brief History of Humankind* before abandoning

   the daydream.

As for the future of Homo sapiens: Welcome to Cyborg Ville.

Who smashed my fucking smartphone?

Five bucks, please.

FISH ON THE DOORSTEP

We fall from the sky into routines.
Some stagger through neighborhoods
engulfed in flames, an unknown
address on the tip of their tongues.
Others recite a cold prayer,
bless themselves
and open a can of beer.
Coherence abandoned,
words split at the seams,
emptying guts of meaning.
Mistakes entrenched;
night stalks shadows.

History books drown
in turbulent waters of the present.
False prophets run scams on the poor,
party on yachts with their ammo and guns.
Televisions drone pundits to those fast asleep.
Nature is a myth; monster storms
and wild fires are illusions –
digital-voodoo, nothing more.
Everything is fine in the duped mind.
Beware the hoax.
Fish on the doorstep confirm
the conspiracy of intelligence.

Celestial Mansions

Everyone knows that death ends the material world.
Some believe we are spirits; the other day
I met an atheistic Christian in the supermarket.
Now it's another day of trying to decide
what I believe.

On television, a TV evangelist pitches
plots of heaven for 3 payments of $19.99.
There are also condos and mansions available.
"For the amazing price of three payments of $19.99!"
the evangelist shouts in a religious sweat. "Call now."

Yesterday, I purchased an electric toothbrush
that detects surveillance bugs in the home for $19.99.
For the same price, I picked up a flexible hose
I can set on fire with a blow torch,
no damage to the hose.

I watch too much television.
But I couldn't function without my $19.99
home grooming and erectile dysfunction kit.
A celestial mansion for three payments of $19.99
is a steal, a heretical bargain.

What's Not Available

- The sex festival in the eyes of a tiger

- Polar ice caps for vacation homes

- Risibility of the present situation

- Words camped in the back of the mind

- Feathers of consciousness threaded through fleecy clouds

- The ability to recognize the alphabet

- Spontaneity of genes

- Dances associated with the Sixth Extinction

- The mystery of kisses in a sealed envelope

- Raindrops lodged in metaphors of tomorrow

- The mud pies from childhood

- Retroactive fantasies in the rearview mirror

- The stone face of despair

- More reasons for not paying attention

- Botox knees and pouty lips

- Fig or Isaac Newtons of imagination

- A clear explanation for not getting it

- What's missing

- What to say

Sky Parlor

Trapped in an attic of clocks.
Some made of fish bones, detritus from the sea.
Others built from animals on the prowl,
snowfalls swift and efficient.
I'm fond of the gold clock of nothingness;
its second hand composed of remnants
from angelic celebrations.
Most record minutes as distant mountains,
howling winds. None keep accurate time.
I've wound them, changed batteries, plugged them
into surge plugs and available outlets.
They ring, yodel and coocoo without purpose.
They're intent on keeping me here,
inside of who I am – bird by nature, soul in flight,
wanderer in the purity of light.

So, Whistle

Invented reality or the IQ of a cloud?
Perfect sense reels in the back room of the unbelievable.
Starlight pure and simple returns to dust.
Follow the footpath in front of you.
That is not an order.
Orders are for diners.
The captains of industry cower.

"Hello" is not a tattoo
Or signal to renew hostilities.
The sky bleeds light.
Now there are plenty of rainbows for everyone.
My dog carries a silver dish in her mouth,
Demands a bone for dessert.
Hammers and saws construct the next dilemma.

The brain is a spasm of words.
Could be a galaxy or a napkin given to wind.
Phone lines of aether.
In the corner of the white room, a piano
A fingerbowl of roses.
The call of the wild, stunted.
Smoke from a cigarette, looming.

The blues infuse electric personalities.
Charm bracelets still popular or not?
Time to discern what just stalled.
The magnificent teapot on the blackened stove.
Book jacket minus the author.
Pigeons, flags and the pharmacy
Closes at 9:00 PM.

The chords of language displace instruments.
Canada geese saunter in the harsh rain.
The city slides into the sea.
News reports rendered useless by the minute.
An armada of asteroids from outer space.
Ceremonies in praise of dawn.
Associations go on sale.

Brilliance in the face of staggering odds.
Memory loss and more available on the Internet.
Nobody likes me.
The unopened letter next to the empty geranium pot.
The summary of mistakes lodges a complaint.
Fragments fragment fragments.
So, whistle.

EXTEND HEAVEN

Today was a struggle –
sky as a series of unopened boxes,
the small print of love
apparently invisible.
I went apeshit reflected the change
in the mind's forecast.

I used to read
The Collected Dialogues of Plato.
Suppose I could leap from body into spirit.
Would I beckon surrealists,
require low wattage lamps
for séance and heartache?
Could I garner a kiss – a smile
not nailed to the predictable?

I have a problem.
The obvious bites me in the ass every day.
Still, I remain a standup guy,
no matter the plane of couch
or therapist's notebook.

Like you,
I've told the ego to take a hike
into the fog of numbers
and deceit.

Lid

I wore the sky as a top hat
to the center of town.
Without clouds, it fit perfectly, once adjusted
for a bird or two in a nest beneath it.
Imagine cardinals, I said to myself.
My mission was simple:

Drop expired medications at the police station,
hurl a suitcase of ideas into a dumpster along the way,
purchase a palette of paints for the next iteration of self.
Citizens offered me a wide berth
when I tipped the sky at them.
Some shielded eyes from a ray gun of photons.

Others snapped pictures with smartphones.
A few requested selfies, which I ignored.
The top hat evaporated into a lovely morning.
A jazz of emptiness bopped in my veins.
Thought improvised nothingness.
Two cardinals flew into the air.

My eyes flamed red with their beauty.
I ascended above the sidewalk
on a cushion of space.
Wings were superfluous.
I returned home to ponder
the nature of reality.

I gazed out my picture window.
A rafter of wild turkeys strutted down the street.
My dog barked at the sound of them.
Quotidian events cluttered the mind.
Rutherford proved atoms are mostly empty space.
It started to rain.

WINGS

Thought shamed transience
into beauty on a day
of calculated missteps

and scam telephone calls.
The knight of roses forgot
to install the fire alarm.

Anarchy seized the streets.
The mind shuffled questions.
What is myth? What is not?

Galaxies burped satellites.
Angelic figures paraded
in shadows cast by prayers –

the text of one written
on the face of the moon.
I burned in the pores of space,

beyond intelligent time.
Sleep bartered darkness
for wings.

LANDING

In the beginning, and there was tremendous debate about that, we fell in love with space as a nutrient. A few of us left or lost the narratives of our lives in the backseats of cars. There were few stats on the meaning of the first few moments. Word crumbs on the floor with assorted beer caps seemed more of a clue about a taste in art, than an insight into the magnificence of an extensive vocabulary.

The veil of meaning moves through language like a lovely ghost. In the streets of yesterday, the progress of clocks lapsed into outright partying. That's how we met. Under the ticking moon of desire, the grand intuition of naming took place. Many held hands and walked down sand sidewalks in the regatta of a full ocean breeze. They needed to escape the screech of tires, cliffs and cunning mathematical detours of tomorrow.

The coals of solitude recorded a different tale. It was a time – remember – of intense form and attention to decay. There was a sense of decoy in the air, not ducks, or moose imitations but more like the absence of fine wine and the confessionals of childhood finally closed. It was a time to laugh, grab the roots of hair left on the head and parachute to safety.

NORMAL DAY

My right thumbnail resembles a pagoda,
my left, an arrowhead.
I track the moon across a fetish of stars.
Beneath a snow-clotted sky, flowers cower.
Scam Likely phones Unknown Caller.
Silence replaces noise with the miraculous.
It's a normal day.

With more guns than people,
America needs more of them.
There should be a stockpile of guns
on every street corner for instant access.
There are so many things coming after us.
You can't be too careful.
It's a normal day.

I walk around with ice bags on my feet,
lie about my age.
The mail arrives with nothing to do.
My vacuum cleaner speaks in tongues.
A rainbow of parrots lives next door.
The escape hatch of belief calms the nerves.
It's a normal day.

Words open windows and scream
at the top of their lungs.
Molecules rehearse chance operations.
A flower in my lapel squirts joy
when I levitate for no reason.
Now absorbs the dialectic.
It's a normal day.

Yellow Tulips

Fatigue sets in
Like a broken watch
On a mountaintop

Cells of body accommodate
Panaceas of fiction –
Employ molecular diction

Words
Do their
Homework

The racehorse
Of synapse
Coughs

The balloon man
Paints
His house

A calypso of birdbaths ranks
Political ideologies
False maps and interior designs

It's time to sip
The martini
Of miscalculation

Wrap
The banner of eternal ideas
Around forlorn dilemma

Freeze celebrity
Compose a sentence
Of finite visions

Without complaint
The sky recedes into a bank
Of yellow tulips

Hostile Reviews

The sun blacked out during a cosmic hiccup. It was an extraordinary
day of two birds, a kite and a whistle. The birds were strangers
to each other. One flew in from New Jersey. The other, burdened
by a single yellow eye, was fond of dissonant chirping. The kite
suffered a brisk wind. The whistle belonged to a fitful god
(representative of the maelstrom of ideas) who orchestrated a quotidian
agenda by reading the book, *Were Did We Go*, stolen from a local library
by a disgraced FBI agent who left it by accident on a crosstown bus
after a failed apprehension of a fugitive on the lam in Lamborghini.

According to the dust jacket, the author of the book lived in Italy
in protest for the lack of understanding of a previous book of his,
Are We Here, had received in America. The book, eschewed
an actual book cover, employing a blank page for it instead.
In exile, the author stated repeatedly and without trepidation,
the blank page cover represented the disappearance of "reality"
in political and social discourse. Critics assailed the book for its audacity
to even mention "reality" and with vitriolic justification called the author
a weasel. One critic went so far as to insist that "reality" did not exist
(much like the book cover) in any objective sense, writing in CAPS:
REALITY IS A FIGMENT OF THE IMAGINATION, BUSTER!

The hostile reviews were too much for the author. Granted,
the book was not a page turner, but the author had zealously described
(without the utilization of CAPITAL LETTERS) the beauty of the earth
and/or "reality" before its wanton destruction by greed, stupidity,
and a collective madness unable to understand the incorrigible rise
in temperature and poor air quality. So, hello, to the art and ancient ruins
of Italy, and thankfully the exiled author's latest work, a fascinating study
of syntax on steroids entitled, *JACKED.* The distraught god (representative
of the maelstrom ideas) stepped off the bus at the next stop. Unconvinced
of a comment scrawled in the book's margin on page 10: *Constant surveillance
of the author is highly recommended,* the deity blew its whistle.

PORTRAIT OF THE ARTIST AS A HORSE AND CAR

I'm a one-legged horse in a field
staring at an apple in a withered tree.
In car language, I'm on my way
to the nearest junk yard, not because
of a specific accident.

You are more comfortable with the image
of a one-legged horse.
Questions are posed:
How do I keep my balance?
Will the horse eat the apple?

In car language, parts are stolen
from cars in junk yards.
Cars are crushed by industrial compactors.
The landscape of junk cars is an eyesore,
suggests a diminution of energy and power.

The one-legged horse retains a modicum of beauty.
My color is caramel.
My mane is dark and thick.
The horse's stallion past is not evident
but can be inferred.

I have won some races,
legit or maybe not.
The car grows into a disfigurement of rust.
The one-legged horse pogoes toward the apple
and crashes to the ground.

Time of Togetherness

I write on napkins in the middle of Avant Garde afternoons. TV on low is a conflict of voices & misunderstood cultures. Easy to say. There was a time of vision – pagan deities & oneness looming – all known – a blue sphere in a black curtain of space.

Are we alone? How did the stock market do today? Some prescriptions cause side effects. You could walk down the street backwards – mess up the narrative of your life. You were an academic star – or at least dreamt the recurring dream of riding a beam of light into the unknown.

Language was never the problem. There were heroes & theories of what you were doing or could do. The moon was out – the moon was a lookout once. Remember? Scratch that collective head. You were in the street with love on your lips like the ultimate kiss. But everything was not OK. You could not defend automatic writing or dispute the latest findings or discoveries by haywire consciousness.

Still, you had a name & thought at times of changing it. Wouldn't that have been something for the rocks of easy living to ponder?

Onomastics

Relax.
The details of your name
are sealed
in a jar
of plums.

Light insists
plums are
juicy & sweet.
But these appear
to be on fire.

This is the metaphysics
of the situation:
You're sorry/not guilty
but have a tendency
to go on about it.

Example: archetypes/
iconic representations of what
nurtures & stimulates, i.e.,
plums outside containment
may be breasts.

Whatever!
Forge what's left of your name
on the bottom line of who
you were (right?).
The jar glows origin.

PRONOUN SOUFFLÉ

1

"They" thought "I"
The lyrical ego
(If "you" must)
Was well past "its" prime
And should retire
Or be retired by
Language

2

Enough with "your" mother's narrative influence – "your" odyssey
      Into the unknown
Or "those" days "you" dreamt of nothing else but being a cowboy riding
      The open range on a Palomino horse with green sunsets
      In "your" eyes

3

Disdain for "you" was tragically revealed
Another pronoun "they" argued
Must be relegated to the dustbin
Of prohibited usage

4

For "whom" is "you" and "who" gives a damn if "it" were a palomino
      Or a Chestnut steed trotting through the archetypical
      Past with thunderous hoofs
As for green sunsets
"They" ("those" in a cowpoke's eyes) may be OK
On some other planet
With the appropriate
Chemical atmosphere ("That" "they" {"them"} were also a "they"

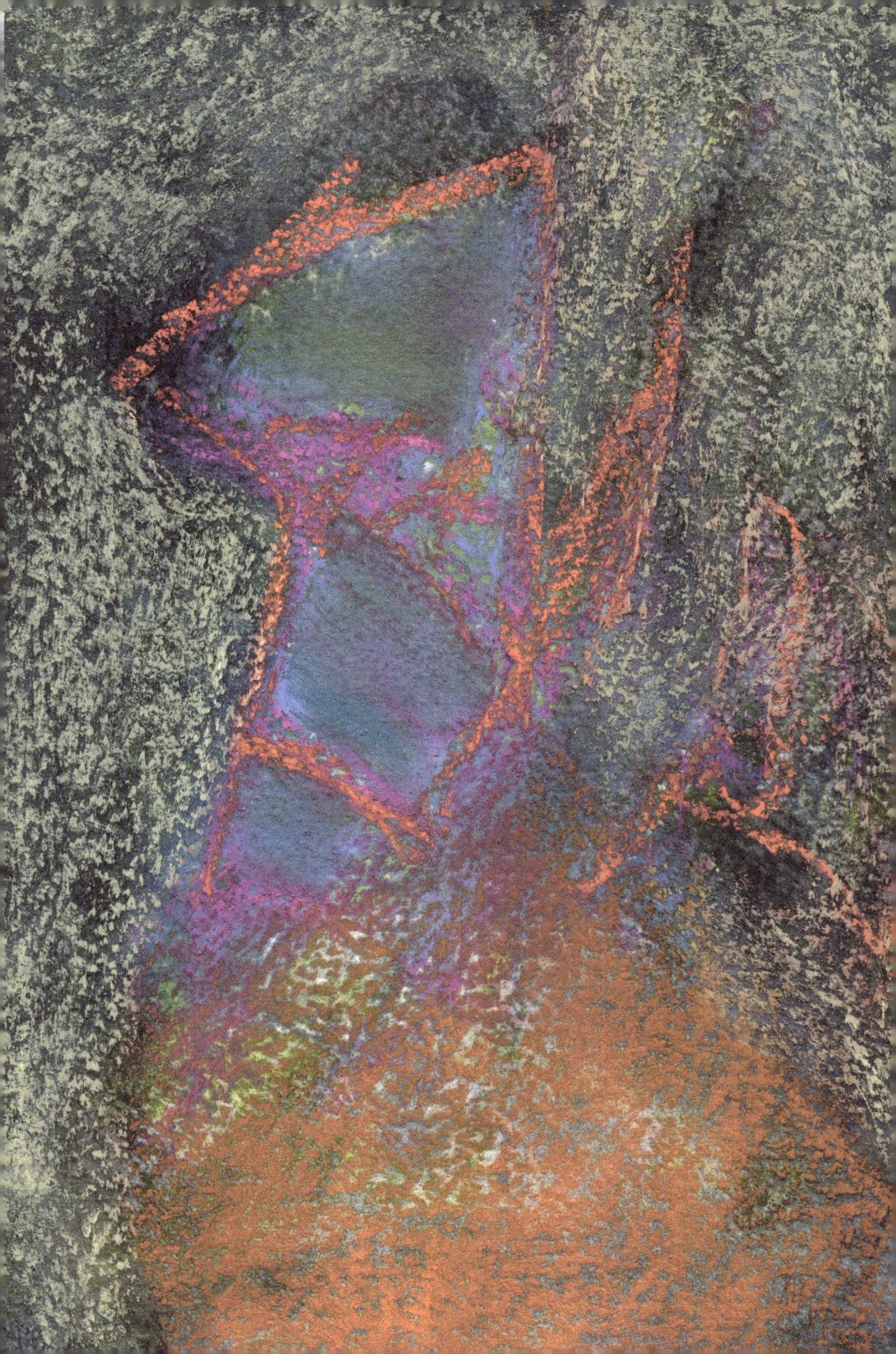

[green sunsets etc.]
And part
Of the pronoun soufflé
Didn't bother "them"
Regardless of the planetary system)

5

Look (meaning "you") "we" think – "they" argued in critical essays – words
        Have the God given right to be unmoored (unhitched cowpoke) from "their"
        Representations (and burden of a lyrical ego) and to be recognized for "what"
        "They" are – composed of letters representing sounds

6

And as "we" "all" know
Sounds are mechanical vibrations
Transmitted through an elastic medium
Traveling in air at a speed
Of appropriately 1087 feet (331 meters)
Per second at sea level
And "these" *vibrations*
(Good – shout out to the Beach Boys)
Are oscillating
Reciprocating or "other"
Periodic motions of a rigid
Or elastic body or medium
Forced from a position
Or state of equilibrium
And in the disguise
Or garments of *words*
Once reaching the ears
Are converted to electrical signals
Riding nerves into the brain
And once processed

I.e., decoded by the brain ("which" by the way has spent years trying to figure out exactly
    "Whom" "it" is in regard to consciousness and consciousness's relationship to the
    Billions of neurons processing "all" kinds of signals including the electrical signals
    Of unmoored (unhitched, wrangler boy) words "that" in "themselves" have escaped
    The burdensome necessity to refer to *something* and thus comprise a world)
May or may not
Disclose meaning
Depending on the attention span of the brain
At a given moment in time

7

Look (see verse 5) "they" have argued words are entitled to "their" "own" lives,
    "Their" own associations "their" "own" peculiar odysseys, "their" own
    Nonreferential worlds and via "those" odysseys compose new
    And alternative vibrating palaces of verbal constructions for the brain
    To decipher and in doing so challenge the stale state of meaning
    In the referential world with "all" "its" cultural political and oppressive
    Baggage "that" resides in the body politic (i.e., community of brains)
    And thus, offer meaning a new contract for Meaning – "one" that permits
    (Honors) no meaning as a meaningful surrogate and consequently
    The lyrical ego – "which" seems to be hanging around despite ridicule
    And threats of death and "who" gives a damn if "its" sorry ass clutches
    To love letters, war, death and divine revelations – must if "it" hasn't
    Already be extinguished and finally put to rest

Sunset On Waves

the exigent
charged body
feeds in a fishbowl
of images
in a dark sky
a blimp of light
scours the heavens
until the myth
of meaning
is reborn
the impresario self

makes the scene
in a thunderclap of applause
and minor gods
the master of ceremonies
taunts geologists to scatter
geriatric rocks in the form
of clues
a feast of archetypes
erupts in the mind
quantum neurons flow
in oceanic thought

beauty quests spontaneity
language dons a subtle disguise
time regresses
into the wails of infants
a cosmic voice reviews
commandments of mystery
and suffering
bodies embrace
in a stew of imagery
sunset on waves
kindles belief

LIMOUSINE HEARTACHE

My mind is a factory of stray numbers.
Mom found me in a basket of eggs on Easter morning.
I am fond of egg salad and bright and friendly dyes.
Some days, I'm as cheery as a crocus.

Alternative facts are big business in the world.
Most say I'm just wasting my life, knitting
Toboggan hats for the Himalayas serves as proof.
The meaning police badger me.

I'm the fork in the road in these parts.
My lover is fine in hers and whole hog about everything.
Drifting in and out memories is a wonderful pastime.
Apocalypse is a favorite topic of conversation at dinner parties.

Nothing comes out of my mouth that is unverifiable.
It is the age of exhausted interpretation.
I hunt for lines in the interstices of make believe.
I am a limousine heartache.

Utopia of Words

Again, I hear you in the meticulous raindrops.
Expect lightning in the soul – the wind
Of yesterday in the trees' dementia.
I mention my backache to no one.

We met under a black umbrella.
How old was I then?
Did I call raindrops tears – reserve a place in my heart
For the goddess of rocks?

A flock of birds peppers the window.
They demand a song – a recitation of sounds
In the notes of my alarm.
My heart pumps music into the room.

Your eyes took me deep sea diving
Into the waters of time.
I wore a secondhand suit and munched on peanuts.
We sold wedding rings for rent money.

The rain picks up;
Your voice is a utopia of words.
I'm an old man with a handheld mirror
And a beef with time.

How many ways have I employed memory
To disclose the details of your face?
Your laughter modified the configuration
Of my mind.

I begin to sing from my arsenal of words –
A cantata of leaves in a fall breeze.
The past bubbles into puddles.
I'm not awake.

I floundered in a torrent of fish and refracted light,
Sought to embrace flowers
As a religious experience.
Incense smoked my eyes.

The rain beats down.
Like you, it must talk to advise.
I won't quibble with words.
Creation resounds in a voice.

Where Have You Gone Joe DiMaggio?

A giant garbage patch of plastic,
twice the size of Texas, floats in the Pacific Ocean
between Hawaii and California.
It contains 1.8 trillion pieces of trash and weighs
about 88,000 tons or about 500 jumbo jets.
A Belgian-American chemist, Leo Hendrik Baekeland,
created the first synthetic mass-produced plastic in 1907.
Polyethylene gained popularity in the 1960s and the movie,
The Graduate, hit the silver screen in 1967.
I graduated from a Catholic High School in 1967.
The lame theme song for the senior prom was "Cherish"
by the Association. I wanted "Light My Fire," by the Doors,
but it didn't get enough first place votes.
I remember Dustin Hoffman (Ben) at the bottom
of the swimming pool during his graduation party
after the single words of advice given to him
by a neighbor: "Plastics."
Charles Webb passed away recently at 81.
He wrote the novel, *The Graduate*, after graduating
from Williams College. He became famous, not rich,
wrote other novels and moved away from *The Graduate*,
living a non-materialist life.
Most of the plastic in the garbage patch comes
from Asian countries with China at the head of the group.
I'm no American angel, still drink water
from single use plastic water bottles.
When I grew up in the fifties, I drank water
from faucets at home and in the park.
No one thought about lead in the brain and the damage
it caused in kids. Everyone smoked; no one wore helmets
when riding bikes or motorcycles.
There were no seatbelts in cars.
Milk came in glass bottles and was delivered
by the milkman to the front or back door.

On November 1, 1952, the US dropped "Ivy Mike"
the first hydrogen bomb on Enewetak Atoll
in the Pacific Marshall Islands.
There's always been an attraction to the cheap
and horrific. Coo, coo, ca-choo!

PRAYER

Memories fly
from my head
into the shattered eyes
of struck deer
I've lost a fortune
in leaves
turned holy boats
adrift on lakes
like missing days
Witness
to what slips
through the cracks
I'm seduced
by the way
words
step from meaning
like a woman
from a dress
at the end
of a hard day
How they peel
off time
shun panties
of sound
and approach me
flashing erotic forms
I live inside
their emptiness
like a lover
who chooses
the cold light
of dreams
for a companion
I'm not to blame
for the lack of substance
Prayer defies weight

ATOMIC DELIGHT

After their annual meeting
the atoms decided they would disassemble,
but would forgo the decision for a time
to allow whomever they were a part of this time
the luxury of getting it together,
before falling apart.
Trillions upon trillions participated in the decision
and felt whomever they composed
would appreciate the courtesy.
In the meantime, hundreds of millions of them
decided to drink heavily and swap stories
about their days as primeval fish in primeval seas,
even the days when they nested on a cold cliff
as a Bald Eagle, caught at times in flight
across a tangerine sunset.
It was a gas being eternal;
but with so many forms available to them,
it felt overwhelming at times.
Though none would complain,
especially on nights they were the moon, coveting
a dark sea before the advent of human beings.
Others, millions and millions and millions
found it appropriate to debate, even argue,
about which mother star gave birth to them.
Having a hot, nuclear mother was cool
and a random occurrence in infinite space.
Arguments ceased, when "Jack" the personality
of their being rolled over in bed, tossed
by a dream of wildebeests on a shopping spree
in a Walmart of artificial Christmas trees
and plots of heaven reduced in price
to a teacup of raindrops.
Religiously, the hundred billion neurons
of the brain were at it again
during the enchantment of sleep,

despite interrupting their Executive Session
on the nature of consciousness
for some surreal entertainment.
On the table for consideration
by the illustrious faction,
before the herd of wildebeests stomped
through their discussion, was consciousness
a mere sensation, an aftereffect
of their electro-chemical artistry,
or something more?
Could it be an immortal soul, member
of an immaterial, spiritual universe
wrapping the entire universe
and subsequent ones destined to appear
like a chain of infinite light bulbs?
Jack didn't know.
But it was time to rise,
brush the teeth,
greet the new day with gratitude
and dazed optimism.

JUMP

As quanta
(And why the hell not)
We reside in a park of light
Fans of incandescent swings

Into the gymnastics off electromagnetic moments
You chuckle lizard
Beams of probability scaffold eternal walls
In a breeze of perfect mirrors, we're the flowers

Let the bottleneck of time break
Words leak fireflies, mystery, a second chance
There are multiple comings
And goings (we appear then don't)

We speak of blue apples and silk headaches
Could use an extra dimension of illusion
Deconstruct nothing into something
Believe in the leaps that got us here

It's difficult to support why we are
So, laugh
Unlike similes for yesterday
We're waves now

THE END OF DETERRENCE

I entered the sanctuary of flowers
with a toothpick in my mouth.
It was one of those mornings
you have sausage for breakfast.
I was pleasantly tired from the night before – the usual
tickertape parade of images – the stardust of maps
sprinkled over everything – signs to the beach
misplaced or stolen for keepsakes by a posse
of former girlfriends, or maybe
landlords.

Sometime after breakfast
I read your letter – sent
months ago by Express mail.
At the time, you were under disguise
in the mountains, had finished a novel
on the history of automatons.
You didn't like the direction of the human world.
It's full of ego and nonsense," you said,
deciding to live off a spontaneous
inheritance in one of your pockets.

The letter was simple enough.
You were out of dough
and could use a few bucks.
Would or could I comply?

There aren't many flowers in my sanctuary.
A squirrel or some rodent chopped off
the head of my only sunflower.
I'm a man of weeds – a man of letters
and charming misreads.
Like the time I wrote the cosmos emerged
from the alphabet.

Talk about controversy!
My only protection from astute detractors –
the moonshine in my pickle jar.

Some days goad me into wearing
a mask for self-protection when I hit the streets
without being there.
Thank God, I was raised on hot dogs
and the writing process.
I know how to edit my beefs:
out of ketchup,
stale rolls,
neighbors with fissile weapons
in holsters, busy
in their gardens.
Security is no longer the issue.

Dear Friend,

It's crazy down here in the valley.
Weeds out number my flowers.
Diet the same.
We're armed to oblivion.
Check enclosed.
Please revise
or advise.

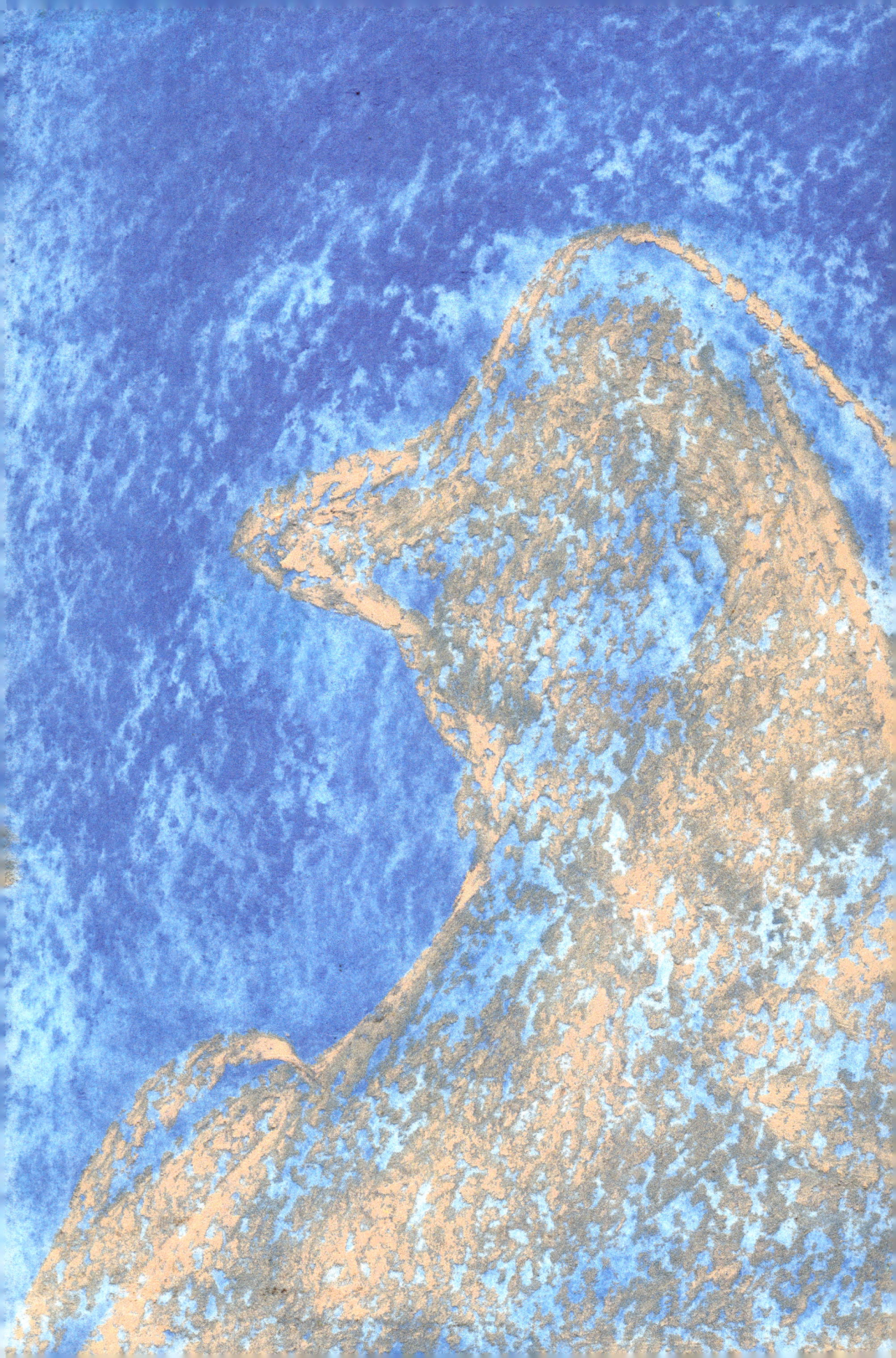

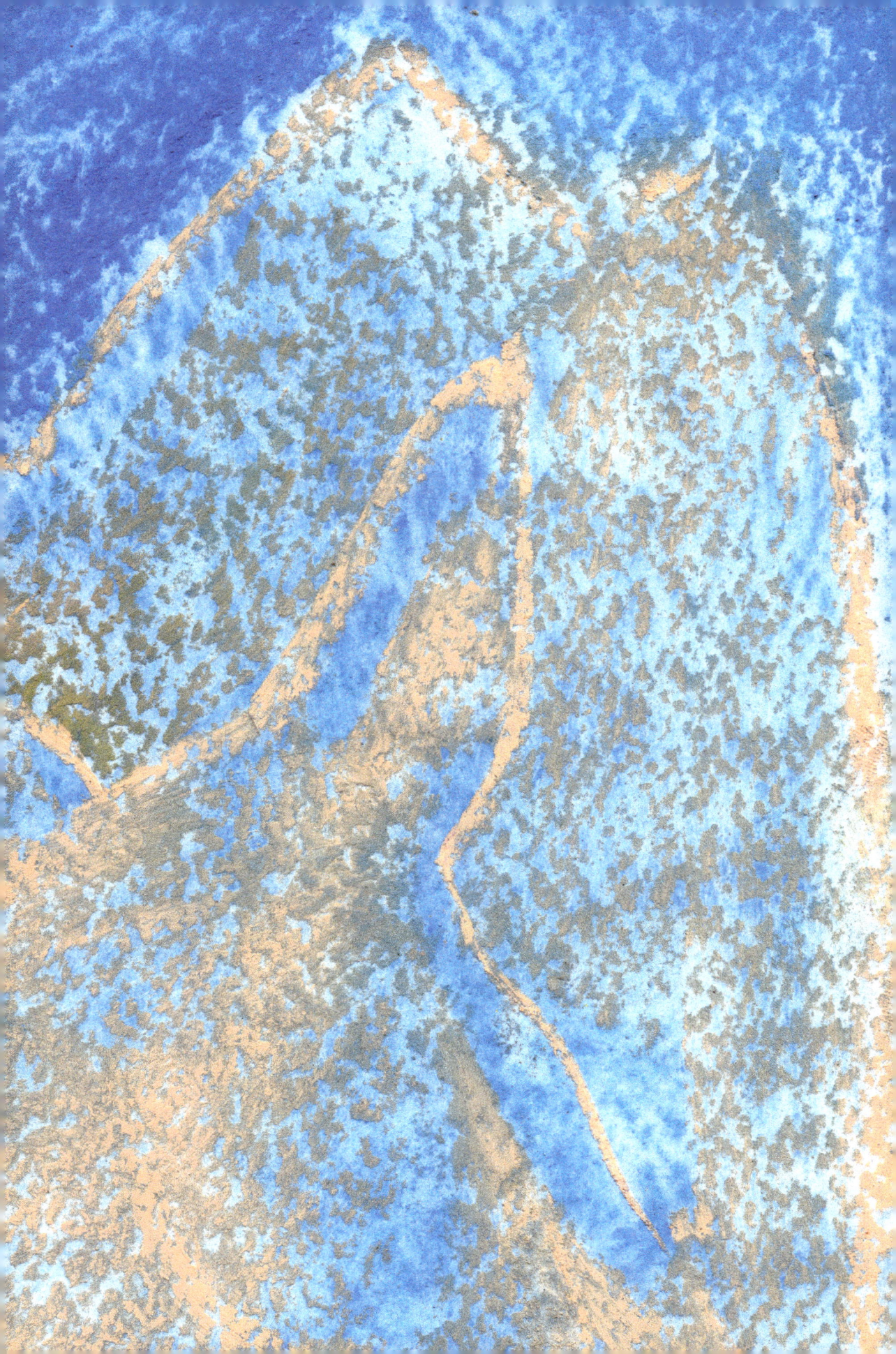

Leakage & Smoke

Words escape from my head,
board a train without a destination,
travel under the black comfort of stars,
a universe bolting nowhere.
Some choose the bar car to debate
their meanings, how they appear
in sentences without permission
or a clear purpose.
Others, engage somnolent passengers
in provocative conversations
about the world, its notorious
condition of neglect due to
profiteers of global capitalism.
I employ their absence to rearrange
my stamp collection of memories –
juxtaposing stamps of tears
and remorse with those laughing
their asses off; placing stamps
lobbing for a group hug next
to one that drowned in moonlight
on the day you said: "We are happy
in our lonely lives together."
But how should I address stamps
from the deep past – those postmarked
heaven or hell, reward or punishment,
those leaking from the unconscious,
as fires flare in postmarks of fear?

PANDEMONIUM

Language absorbs the night

Mind is a lonesome angel

I've heard of terrible and good ones   those in fabrics

those in astral corrals   Thought generates

an electric polis   So much for desire

I left my fonts in San Francisco   Where

exactly is the Theater of Paradise

Yes   a pristine hollow formed in time's advantage

Game on   you could say

Signs for labyrinth abound   rebound

in a triceratops of sunlight   Party on

evolution   you should say

Yo   dancing head   will you cause a ruckus

in the neighborhood tonight

WIRELESS PARADE

for xj dailey

wind

    or the stirrups of bad luck

my toaster oven has canceled all Public Appearances

    be infamous will ya

theories of diction & etiquette distain

    the informality of mob rule

however   X napped on extinct railroad tracks

    during a season of blue mermaids

nine11

    or the moon of retired desires

the façade of obsequious landlines stirred consternation

    in objects of planned obsolescence

    P A Y or P L A Y   A T T E N T I O N

    you've been digitized

good news

    or warts of consciousness

tests indicate that your only risk factor is your age

When the Obese Police showed up at the door

The Empire of Spare Change demanded transparency

your place

  or the polis of my mistakes

under the duress of timelessness

  historic moments plummet in value

why not claim

  thought is a wireless parade

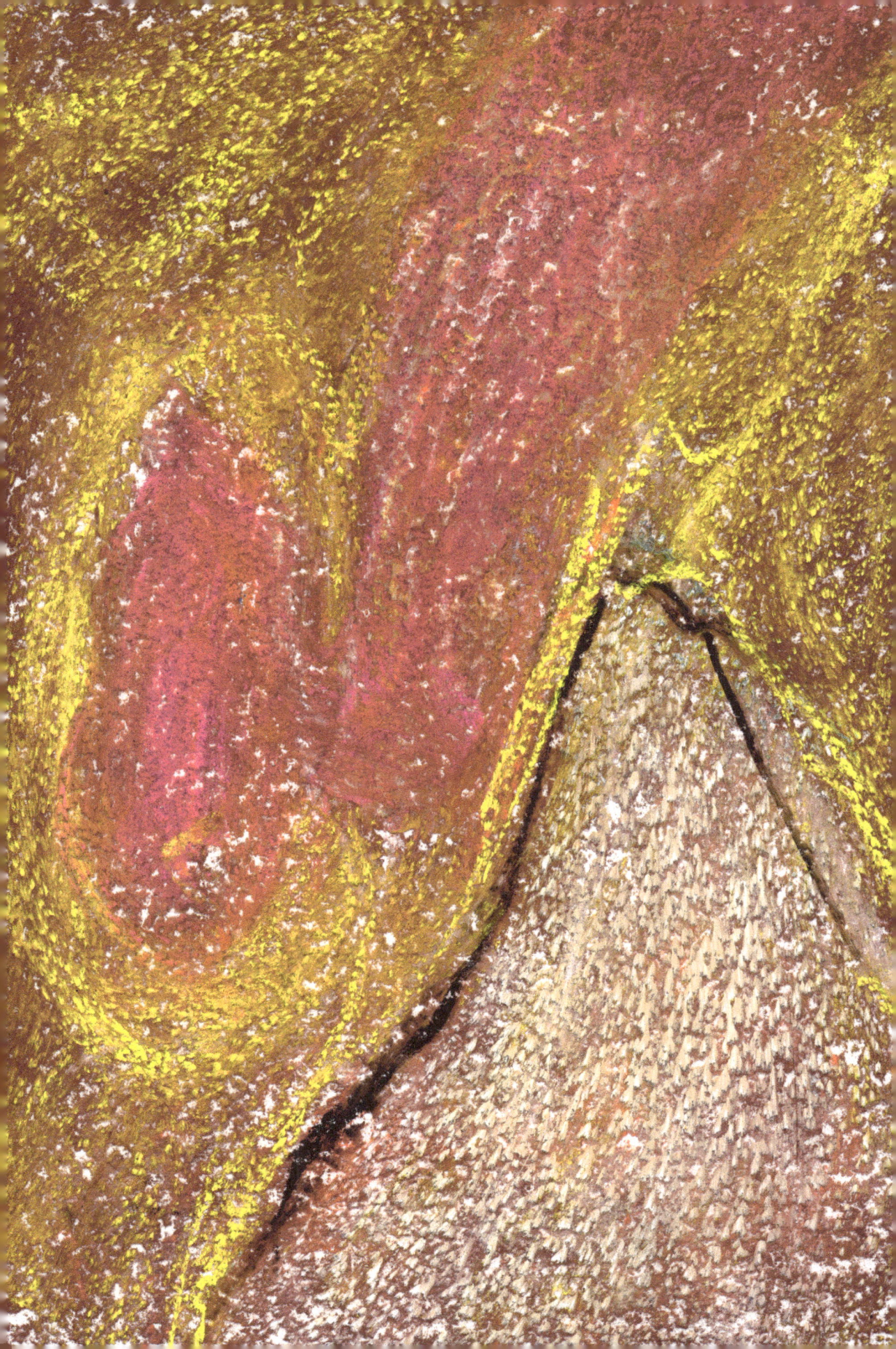

BIRDS SANG WILDLY

I watched as darkness swung
over the fading light
and landed in my backyard.
It was hungry – munched
on tufts of winter grass,
final patches of snow.
It was tired – demanded
trees fill with birds,
for them to sing wildly
as it flashed a bellyful
of crimes.

I thought it might be time for supper
or to take the dog for a walk.
I considered offering darkness a drink –
a scotch or bottle of foreign beer.
Things in the world weren't going so well.
Innocent people were being killed for no reason,
including children playing with toys.
There was talk on tv of nuclear extinction,
still praying to God, as the old earth
lumbered around a yellow star
with madmen and generals.

Darkness took to scotch like a baby a bottle
consumed half of the fifth before I cut it off.
It babbled vehemently, threatened
and collapsed into a drunken ball of night.
I remember the streetlights wept
as it rolled beneath them.
Birds sang wildly.
I woke up.

BILL OF SAIL

The totality of now
is eternal
sounds preposterous
The ball game is on

and the physics
of the fastball has
your name on it
So where is meaning

in the stats of darkness
I have entered the wind
once or twice to relocate
as a scuffed seed

I'm thankful for water
sun and the chance
to grow from under a rock
into a conversationalist

That's how I met you
on a stranded beach
with stones in socks
weathered smile

Remember the waves
rinsing our feet – syllables
of surf advanced
contentment

how our minds merged
as distant boats
eclipsed the horizon
of time's deceit

MELODY OF DISAPPEARANCE

I set the mind on fire
to watch its myriad forms, burn.

Saint   Sinner   Spirit   Soul

It's the process (I'm into).
Something to do on a day clouds
are dump trucks of sky, impatient,
to drop loads of weather on earth.

Rain

Hailstones

Ermine coat of snowflakes to clothe barren branches of trees

Bolts of Zeus

A standing ovation of thunder

Heated, the mind skips like a stone
across a slate-sibilant ocean. Plays god
and goddess without regret, sparking
infinite ripples into oblivion.

But I infiltrate the head of pin
with a flock of nameless angels.
The snapshot of it, faded, shriveled
into a package of dust, invisible phoenix
in the melody of disappearance.

Rain

Hailstones

Ermine coat of snowflakes to clothe barren branches of trees

Bolts of Zeus

A standing ovation of thunder

But I imbibe the smoke of combustible syllables,
an ideology of sound in the morning light.
Birds sweetly in my ears,
informing me of notes
I fail to hear.

The mind leaps and pirouettes
in light and darkness,
orchestrates metaphysical particles
into the symphony of becoming.
But I tune a singed horn.

Rain

Hailstones

Ermine coat of snowflakes to clothe barren branches of trees

Bolts of Zeus

A standing ovation of thunder

THE MOON'S BALCONY

Buoyed by absurdity, I returned
to the scene of the crime.
Someone had stolen one of my shoes
and fingered my street organ.
Bystanders encouraged me to move along.
The corner I stood on was reserved for rioters
and insurrectionists – those manipulated
by political elites who lived in gated bunkers,
fat on wealth, brandishing Ivy League degrees.
I had a stomachache with the intensity
of a Big pathological Lie about election fraud,
complimented by a strong desire
for an egg salad sandwich.
I loved egg salad sandwiches but trembled
when I read in *Conspiracies for Dummies*:

The ingestion of an egg salad sandwich
during an intestinal disorder event
allows anarchists to overthrow
backyard barbeques and serenade
lonely hearts languishing on the moon's
balcony with homemade guitars.

There were other conspiracies described
in the fetid pages of the book.
A fair amount of people believed
Jesus had returned to earth as a gold icon
in white buck shoes and coiffed hair.
He loved to cheat at golf,
consult his own big brain
when it came to grave eternal matters.
A professional conspiracy theorist on my street
informed me that he Q-ed my neighbors
via Facebook I had been abducted by aliens,

forced to endure the effects of limping around
with one shoe on and one shoe off, claiming
someone had fingered my street organ.
And that's why he was armed and had to be.
"A shoeless foot was one thing," he said.
"The street organ was a fucking nuisance."

When Truth Disappears

I'm accustomed to the facts uttered by strangers

Mosquitoes detect bad breath

Flies taste food with their feet

What is the difference between a blank page

and a tsunami of absence

We are all brilliant in digression

I heard on the radio (*the sound salvation*)

We're now in the Golden Age of Neuroscience

Know thy synaptic self

When a horseshoe crab digests its dinner

its neurons assist the process

with a symphony of white noise

There's a warrant out for my arrest

Am I missing something

Deep Water

Yesterday, I went for a swim in the unconscious.
There were no yesterdays there.
Time sat alone under an apple tree in full blossom.
It seemed content enough not to move
Or acknowledged my presence.
Zeno's arrow clutched in its teeth.
The archetype factory was in full production.
Primal mom and dad gave me the thumbs up.
Kind of strange.
With not much to do, I skated on an ice pond
Suspended in midair.
Midair was nearly a theme.
I noticed a bag of dreams on a park bench
Levitating in the middle of a blue sky.
It was an ordinary bag, a brown, paper one,
Favored by grocery and supermarkets.
Could my dreams be in that bag?
I've had good ones and bad ones.
The other night, I swerved to the right and left
With a emerald-eyed goddess on a fiery motorcycle
In a musical melody of slippery roads
And blinding snow. She enticed me
With a cabin she said she built on a mountaintop
Free of the mundanity of telecommunications
And the onslaught of info-entertainment.
I slipped off my bed in my readiness,
Sustaining a slight bruise in the temple area.
Her laughter echoed in my head.

I didn't know where I was in the unconscious.
It seemed opposed to maps and satellite GPS.
I felt a slight sense of place underwater
With fish that spoke in an excited stream
Of phosphorescent bubbles.
A language of beauty surfaced

As Orion hunted in the silver night.
There were speedboats of terror
Circling like sharks.
Sharks were part of the deal.
I gained the shore
Because it was there
Without warning.
I wasn't sure what to make
Of the bonfire of memories.
Were they mine spiraling
In sparks into the night,
Feed for the unknown.
I accepted the warmth offered.
A few bottles of whiskey materialize
In a congregation of souls, clamoring
For a good time around the fire.
With a few rounds hammering my brain,
I begged my leave and walked along
The beach, gathering seashells.
With a necklace of them
Around my neck,
I reentered the water.

BRILLIANT SKIES OF STARS

We are made of the substance that created us. The substance which composes our theoretical imagination & sets & resets the ongoing limitations of it as it vibrates in mysterious ways, creating the mythic particles of daily life.

You may be sunbathing in it right now, rowing across one of the seven seas listening to the radio & the cries of gulls, or even noticing that the body while aging will not fly off the surface of its intent like balloons & helium feathers, which in their own birthrights are ruled by magnificent forces of cohesion & coherence.

Sometimes it appears that the substance, which seems like such a ridiculous word for something so non-substantial, doesn't play at getting it right, once it settles on an evolutionary path.

On the surface of things, it can make mistakes, encode wrong or partial information & lapse into forgetting that it is the substance after all – the the main ingredient of all things. But even in loops of conundrum & forgetfulness, it fuels brilliant skies of stars to stay the call of the sirens of entropy.

ENLIGHTENED SYLLABLES

Buddha sits under
The marvelous Bodhi Tree
Free of all desires

It's all ego for some
Basho's frog leaps into the void
Good morning collapses

Candles flicker out
Bathing in the soul's darkness
Clouds shroud moon and clock

Room of fire and books
Bundled tight in solitude
Almost time for lunch

Who is the witness
The sound of one hand clapping
Heron stares from pine dock

Talk about process
Pain harbored inside storm clouds
Body drenched in time

Still branches and snow
The wind loves a holiday
Mind shivers freedom

Eight haikus this week
Lost self in a pile of nouns
Love romantic verbs

A Poem for Dr. Blossom

In Memoriam Peter Kidd

There's a time when the mind grows silent,
finds its metaphysics in birds chirping in trees,
light dancing on leaves in a gentle breeze.
Years ago, you put me on your plant crew.
The reason you gave was because
I handled them like they were alive
as I unloaded them from your truck.
That was a start, hauling mulch
in a wheelbarrow, my job.

I needed to dig into the earth, smell it,
get bit by black flies – only the earth
could heal the mind. Flowers and bees,
the blossoms all around us had for centuries
perfected the best therapeutic techniques.
The mind had to get dirty, sweat and swear
to become visible to itself. To comply,
I dug holes, planted lilacs and day lilies,
mulched and watered them.

Cancer invaded your body four years ago.
Your fight to beat it was fierce.
You never stopped writing or laughing.
There were times in the Texas heat,
we sat on your porch, considered
your prized roses in shared silence.
A damselfly came to rest on the tip
of one of your fingers.
Nature knew who you were.

You lived in two other worlds coexistent
with the visible one.
Everybody who loved you realized
you were a triple threat.

In the second world, you said your soul
was a high-flying acrobat bound
for earth many times before.
Death did intrude on the eternal,
challenge the community of souls.

We shared our poems and smoked a joint.
Stars dropped into sight.
A chill called for a blanket on your knees.
The third world was neither visible
nor spiritual. It was not binary.
That gig was up.
This world contained matter,
energy and spirit, entering and leaving
your body one breath at a time.

You toked heavily on the joint.
I watched the exhaled smoke curl
into the air and vanish.
Something like that, you said.
It was time to retire – another treatment
scheduled for tomorrow.
There may be a fourth world, you offered,
standing and opening the screen door.
For now, enjoy the stars, friend.

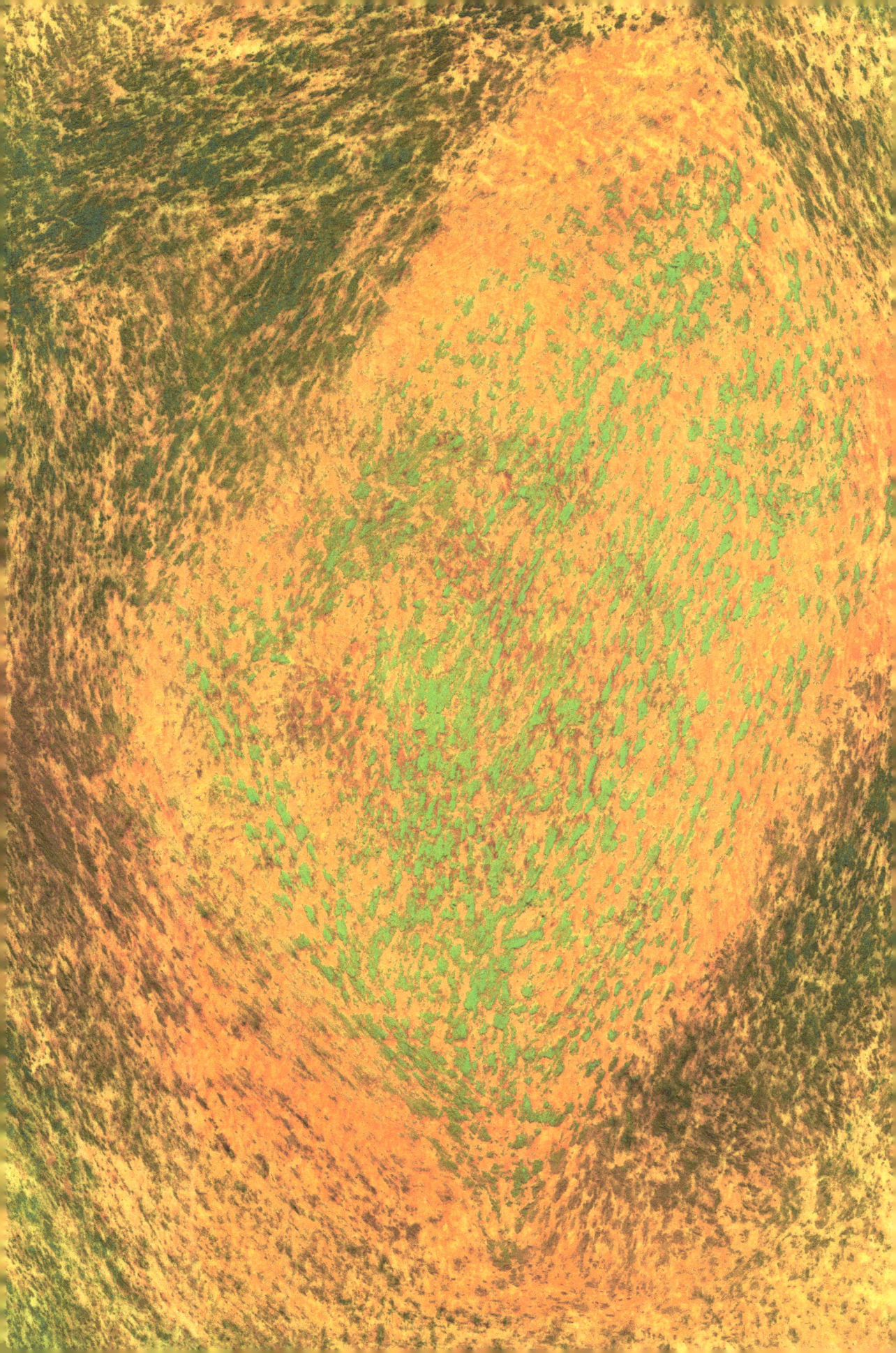

Give It a Try

Bring nothing.
A lover on a bank of roses waits for you.
Let the rocks and water of a hidden spring
sedate you with their music.
You were here long ago, perhaps
in another life. Who knows?
Who should know?
Banish clothes, reenter the water,
embrace the moment. Remember?
The night grows lovely with moonglow.
Don't ask why.
The world outside is beautiful
but broken in many places.
People have turned sticks and stones
into missiles and bombs,
other gadgets of self-destruction.
They have turned green into brown.
Domes of fire halo their heads.
Lies haunt their speech.
It is cool where you are.
A forest of love surrounds you.
Time is that moment you forgot.
Imagination is eternal.
Give it a try.

LETCHWORTH STATE PARK

for Tom Haines

How many steps must we take
before feeling the ground of eternity
beneath our feet
Look at the mud on our shoes
Fresh mud
April mud
Cruelest alluded to mud
of clay selves
thick and gooey
packed with red pine needles
last year's leaves

Days of hard rain have passed
The roar inside me
is the Genesee River
muddy and wild
in a series of thunderous falls
billowing falls
falls with the angle mist
and sunlight
to sprout
(Like moss – deep green moss
thatched
into a face
we recognize {for it is us now}
as a god
natural and austere
mostly sad
or maybe just patient
in the eons
it feels
as rocks – the very rocks
of its Being)
a rainbow

The Seneca called these falls
Sehgahunda: vale of three falls
thought the Middle Falls –
Skagadee – so beautiful
the sun stopped each midday
to admire their beauty

We're outside
But when inside the head
(You say)
the torrent of water –
water from winter snows
and recent rain
water
tons of it – majestic
with a slight yellow tinge to its brown
chocolate
Soul
is us
not just you and me
but
us
the *them* we all know
in cars on interstate highways
in office cubicles
walking crowded streets
no longer able
to hear roaring rivers
or consider
endless stars
(Consider the word
"consider." It's root
you explain
comes from *sidereal*.
Once "consider"
meant to pause,
look at the stars,
but when we do

there's a haze
from ubiquitous city lights.
The infinite stars, dull
and murky swim
in a fishbowl night
unnoticed)

Them then
us
you and me
we
plunging over the falls
the falls
our very bodies
blasting
off rocks
into a turbulent abyss
Each instant of water
an instant of self
memory
joy
fear
passion
riding the falls
in individual or collective barrels
alone or together
with others to follow
in the billowing mist
as those ahead of us
cut deeper into our rocky
ancestral home

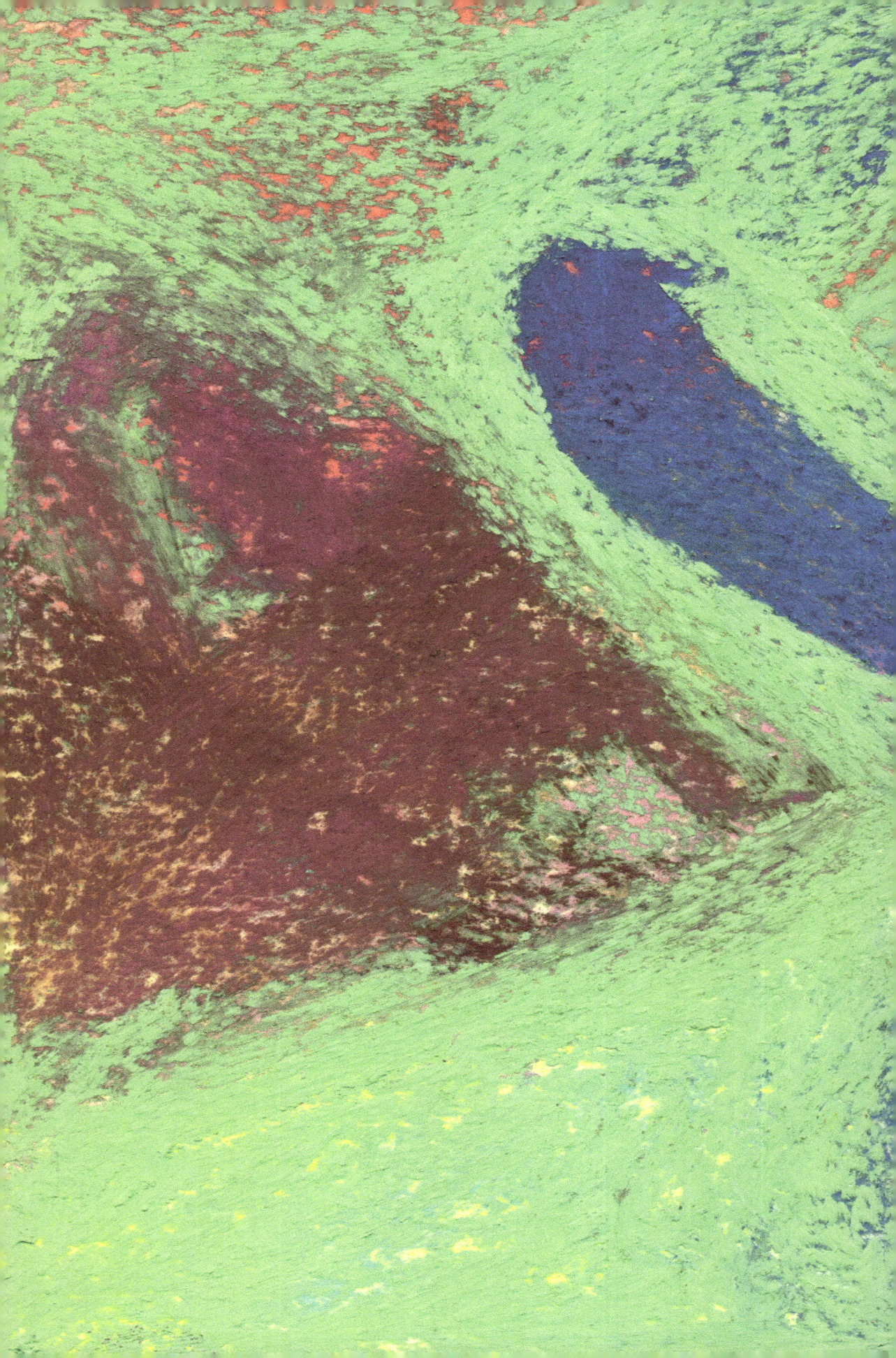

MYSTERIUM INTERRUPTUS

We were in a dream,
shoveling snow & busy
imitating a symphony of birds
on a transiter radio.

"No explanations as per request," you said.
"Write the love letters you promised."

> Dearest X,
>
> Like you, I am fond of expensive
> wines & abstruse conversation.
> I am enthralled by your beauty,
> polish my words into mirrors
> for the soul. I flash my Plato
> Fan Club Card as neighbors
> turn into strangers.
>
> Hats off to Larry,
>
> A

Dearest Y,

So, you've changed your name
from X to Y. I majored in Onomastics
in college, developing an acute
fondest for names associated
with love and beauty – Aphrodite,
Bella, Amor etc. Y means all
of these to me.

> Did you know heaven adores
> the invisibility of dark energy?

Who wrote the Book of Love?

B

Dearest Z,

The alphabet can't keep me from you.
I am addicted to "letters" & enticed
by your flashy body & fleshy lips.
BTW, my last foray into the majesty
of clouds left me heartbroken
& without wings.

O, the holy electromagnetism of it all!
I built a house of light to honor you.

Goo goo g'joob

C

Dearest X, Y &/or Z,

I love the mystery
of not knowing
if I know you.
Is that you banging on
the door of our dream?
My exhaustion for you
is incomplete and transparent.
I live in the iconic moments
of an imagined presence.

Welcome! to the body of this letter.
It has been waiting for you
without complaint or signature.

PS   I have sealed my guilt
         in stardust dogmas
                  falling into the sea.

Cubicle Soliloquy

Exiting a maze of memory boards,
I entered a town whose gold-eyed inhabitants
shed mirrors of distance during elaborate conversations.
At the intersection of A and -A, a cloud of timeless clocks
hovered above me like a portal to eternity.
While considering my options, the mayor emerged
from a sunflower in a garden of angels.
Over cocktails during a rainstorm of rainbows, she explained
the mantra of the town, its raison d'être for existing.
A woman of no particular age, her golden eyes gleamed, kindness.
Periodically, schools of colorful fish swam through her,
until replaced by a staccato of sunsets without warning.
"You see in this world," she said, "we honor the transience of beauty."
She handed me a satin envelope and excused herself
due to a prior engagement. I opened it and read:
Get your head into the game and see if you know your meditation
facts with this mindfulness quiz. PS LOL.
When my manager clipped me on the back of the head,
my laugher ceased. A faint glimmer of hope flickered
on my laptop's screen.

Antidote Metric

We all have stories,
were born under this or that
star system or sign.
It was a beautiful day.
It snowed like hell.
Mom cuddled us or didn't.
Dad maybe drank too much,
went off to war – the interminable
wars of the species
in electromagnetic fluctuations
of ignorance.
Religion ignited the war inside of us.
The world drifted between heaven and hell,
cruised through an eternal mind,
presented a veil of forms
that fooled the eye:
mountain ranges,
meadows,
cloud formations,
the slap of ocean waves on shore,
a slap in the face, remember?
How old were we then?
Did the weather or flowers care?
Was it raining?
Where did we hide?
Was it before or after the Bomb
on history's clock?
Were we rebels with a cause
or without one, modernist
or postmodern shoppers?
Who didn't love shopping online?
Who cared if Media deformed us –
ruse of corporate Reality
to sell products delivered
by drones and robots

to the front door?
It was just business when hackers hacked,
sold phone chargers that exploded
like baked apples during virtual games,
as our homes burned to the ground.
Maybe this was not our story.
Our story was locked in a posthumous vault.
We were caught with our hands in the till,
rejected commandments of radical finitude.
Lovers and children shook us awake.
The world was a merry-go-round,
a summer day without end,
a flyball launched into nowhere
at the speed of light.
We were multiplicities, possibilities
of the possible, weren't we?
We were there during the death of God,
(Why didn't prophets get along?)
the author's demise, when politicians
embraced the ecstasy of division,
when glaciers soaked our feet
and chilled our knees, when children
looked at us, wondering what they could do.
We were there as stories,
telling them now.

Chameleon Outtake

The mind grieves in a catalog of mistakes;
I can't find boots or overcoat.

Oceans evaporate in a fit of snowflakes;
I'm lost in the sound of your voice.

Things smell fishy in rabid moonlight;
I draw the ace of hearts from a deck of words.

Hypnotic night assumes responsibility;
I smash my smartphone.

Logic succumbs to a change in temperature;
I suture tears in the fabric of space.

Numbers breed conversation;
My body stands in a doorway of ghosts.

Language creates a maze of interpretation;
I am suit of changing colors.

BIG SECRET

*

Love appeared as a statue.
"Take it," I said.
"It's for you."

*

The house of parrots fell under suspicion.
Neighbors peered through windows
into a prism of light.

*

Your body covered mine like a lampshade.
I offered an umbrella of shadows
just in case.

*

Planes roared overhead.
Squirrels played tagged with the wind.
Everything had some bop in it.

*

The cat was on the porch.
Where did it go?
The dog sniffed a quantum tail.

*

No one would say
if I had been reborn or not.
It was a big secret.

Goodnight California

in salt clouds
and palms
the moon rises

pink infant voice

the Pacific howls
creeps

an adjustment
of sense
takes place

time is blue
empirical
cool to the feet

ankles drenched in a coreless past

the Red Nerve Express flies
through tunnels of flesh
desire flows

sparks of foam
schizophrenic beach

you breathe the air
smell the electric wars
of primitive fish

think of happiness
or a friend's sharp pain

a pelican glides toward oblivion

each one has a way
of looking
at the sea

rehearsing
retreat

QUIVER

The sun descends
Into a salmon pond
Fairly large
Some cry ocean
There are waves
Crashing distant shores
Mental ones
Footprints in the sand
Broken shells
Lovers on dunes
Of memories
A last kiss preserved
In sea glass
Yellow fins of light
Belong to other fish
They swim in an open
Sea of sky
Is faith commensurate
With reality?
The body walks
With its faithful dog
Dog pulls on the leash,
Steps into the road
To sniff a stain shaped
Like an irregular polygon
The body waits
In a sphere of silence
What time is it?
Darkness checks its watch
Will the play start on time?
Cars turn on headlights
To chastise twilight
Stars rehearse
The body squints
Theatric trees don a rose shawl

The wind sleeps in the mind
There is nothing
For it to do
Why is there something
Rather than nothing?
Hours ago, the body
And mind were one
Wind chimed shriveled
Leaves, hanging
From a winter branch
The body walks
With its faithful dog
Allows the imagination
To ascend into a sky
Beset with loneliness
And electric nerves
Other things:
A trio of garbage cans
Left in front of a house
A black cat on a stone fence
Conjures the moon
There it is, rising in back
Alleys of the mind
The body walks
With its faithful dog
How is there something
Rather than nothing?
Shy neighbors
Tucked in their homes
The play begins
With snowflakes
The body quivers
With excitement
Dog spots a rabbit
Lines recite themselves

Could Be the Process

Step 1:   Smash the language of social reality into a thousand pieces with a glancing blow of the head.

Step 2:   Randomly blindfold ten language fragments. Remove blindfold and eat a tuna sandwich made with Hellmann's Real Mayonnaise for lunch.

Step 3:   Compose a line using the ten fragments: *The ancient manifesto in the willow tree dines on cheese.*

Step 4:   Perform the same exercise 100 times. Compose a one-hundred-line poem. Read blindfolded. Consider the gallery of invisible meanings.

Step 5:   Accept you're a master and ignore the literary establishment.

Step 6:   Hire protection.

Step 7:   Bask in the knowledge you've brought language back to life. Just like Lazarus. Play Powerball.

Step 8:   Ignore steps 1-7.

Step 9:   Stay disengaged from reality.

Step 10.   Knit a pair of discontinuous socks.

SOMETHING

Consciousness is made of holes
I heard this before
Maybe said it
Sensed it's stored somewhere
in the archives of the brain
Maybe it matters
Maybe it doesn't
This morning a flock of blackbirds
entered my mind
They fed on lawn seed
put down on the yard
by my wife yesterday
I don't remember what
I did yesterday
There were possibilities
to consider

I caught an oak leaf
wrapped in sunshine in my hand
a squadron of them in the air
showing off in a brisk wind
I compared the vein pattern
in the leaf with the palm lines
in my other hand
a pointless exercise
though my love and life lines
would benefit from analysis

                                    Or

I sat on the front porch
sipping Jameson's whiskey
from a crystal whiskey glass
You have to have the right glass
for Jameson's especially when
waving at passing cars
now and then chasing one
up or down the street

pacifying the dog in me
Maybe it matters
Maybe it doesn't

Or

I knew in my bones
something was up
when later that night
I received a text message
alerting me that my medical data
had been breached
It was possible
some hacker or group of them
would have access to the exact date
of my hernia operation
They could easily use
my social security number
to claim they had
my hernia operation
felt some pain
even a pinch now and then
biking in the rain
lifting ten-pound weights
in the cellar

Plus

easy pickings to half
a dozen other various ailments
internal organs even
"Water" pills for the bastards
I best enroll immediately
in one of the many
identity protection agencies
to prevent further theft
of what had gone haywire
in me

So

I decided to take a walk
in the moonlight wearing
my favorite sunglasses

Thoughts played pinball
in my head
Maybe it matters
Maybe it doesn't
At the very least
it was time to patch holes
in my consciousness
with something special
A few abstract paintings by a friend
A documentary or least a video
of a flock of blackbirds
flying in and out of my mind
The memory of a hug and a kiss
on a cold winter's night

                                        Or

Something

Transient Passage

A rose blooms in a glass vase,
roots buried in yesterday's garden.
People enshrined in protective gear
discuss the fate of time, unaware of my presence.
Birds, adorned in primary colors,
fly around the room.

Will it rain today?
Will clouds fulfill the promise of limited conversation?
Many questions are no longer relevant in the arena of politics.
Who won? Who lost?
Who missed the history books by a nose hair?
Let it rain.

It's time to address those hacking the offshore
accounts of the rich and infamous.
Salient points to deliver:
    1. Mind sways in an afternoon breeze.
    2. Love enters and exits imaginary windows.
    3. Metaphors abandoned without cause.
    4. Proceed.

What is real now?
Eyes consume light years of stars.
Almost visible, I emerge
in the beauty of life, catching
the bloom.

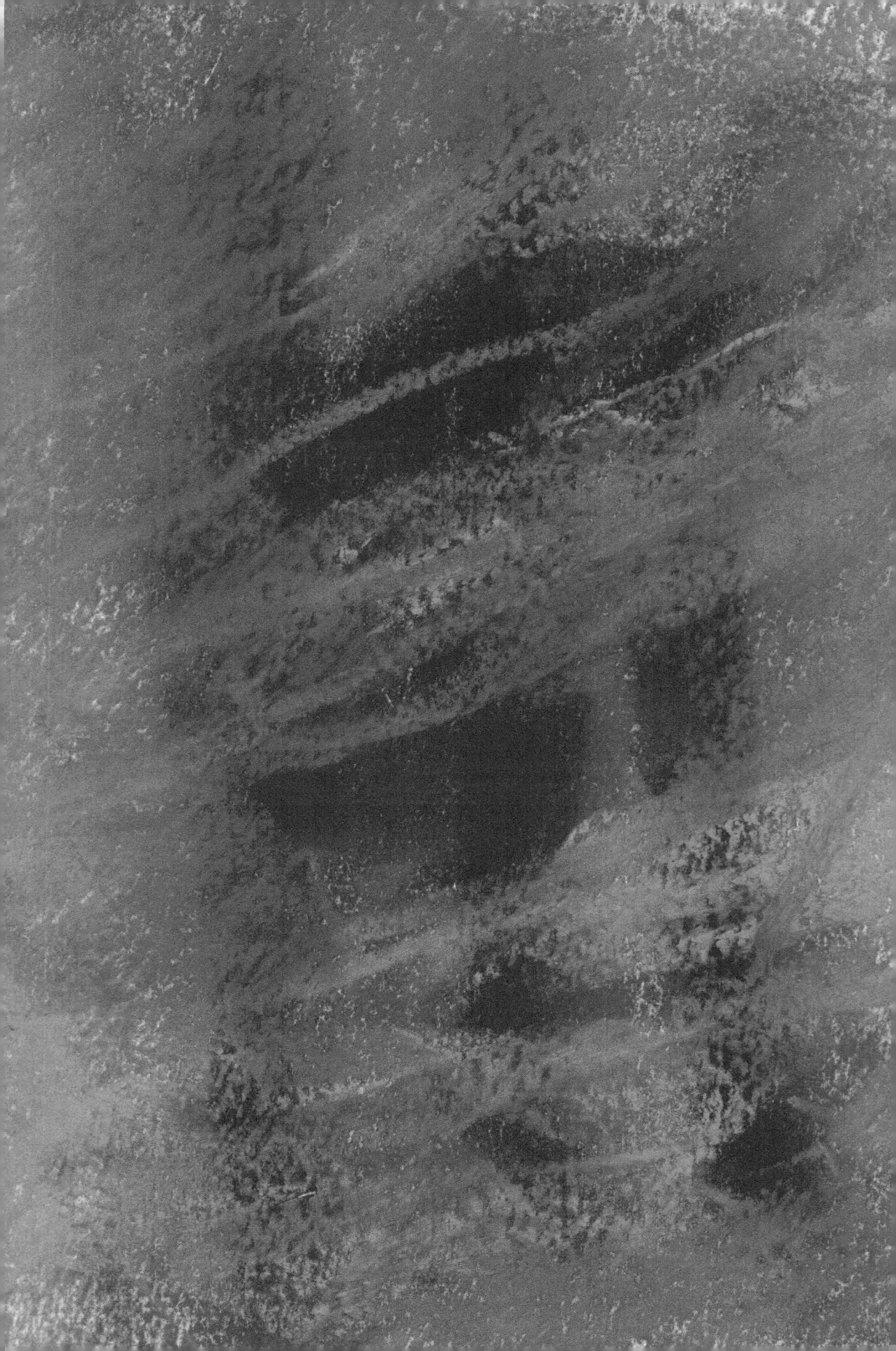

BRIEF SAGA

for Eileen

1

The day the sun
burnt a hole
in my head
      and filled it
      with radiant
      particles
I told
      my doctor
      that
      I
      was
      an eccentric
born in a hot air balloon
      over the Indian Ocean

2

There are too many pill commercials
on TV
      I can't keep up with the side effects

Once I took a fastball
in the nuts
      for standing at
home plate
      like a hopeless
      existentialist

3

Light is wonderful
I just heard on the radio

it rains diamonds
   on Jupiter

The past is littered with mistakes

   We met under an
apple tree
   didn't we
4

This is just to say

I pinched
the faux pas
teetering on
your tongue

and which
you were probably
trying to save
for the right occasion

Forgive me
it was deliciously
inappropriate for dealing
with polite society

5

There are various telescopes
   fixed on the universe
Imagine the one buried
   under the surface
of the Antarctic icecap to detect
   neutrinos traveling
from the sun through the center
   of the earth

6

Hold my hand
       as we surf
light's radiant waves

TOMBSTONES IN SPRING

The green space between tombstones caught my eye
Wine unsatisfactory   a sprig of lilac in your hair
You loved me like a tough yesterday   Whitman believed
It was as lucky to die as to be born

Movement was everything   the speed of conversation
Light beam of immortality   O to be fantastic
& in perpetual motion   You were here in the not here

Of it all   alone in not being alone   We catered beauty
To each other   buzzed to a standstill in the traffic
Jam of love   I was a ghost of perception   a tree

In a pagan forest   collage of disguise   Spared
The amphetamine criticism of the differences
Between us   pen on page   language passed
Through the antiquity of bones

Manifesto in Absentia

1. My poetry services the variegated personalities of consciousness.

Exempla:

Are animals depressed on religious holidays?
Quiet sleeps in the bones of revelation.

2. Barbaric yawp owns this line.

Exempla:

I refuse to answer the door or take questions from the studio audience during electric storms and power outages in my omniscient body.

Does the ecstasy of lugging huge parcels through humid subway tunnels, after an interminable day at the office, vanquish sensibility?

3. It's Howdy Doody time.

Exempla:

Do verbs prefer uber vehicles for transport?
I have a pet quark.

4. Luminaries of form enjoy Synapse Karaoke on Friday nights.

Exempla:

We're in trouble as a planet.
Is nothingness a deity or a Hit Parade of subatomic particles?

5. Love is the metaphysical constant in electromagnetic radiation.

Exempla:

Is there a (only the) lonely inside of me?
Moon daisies reflect an amorous light.

PHARMACEUTICALS

Time defeated,
I sleep under the umbrella
of a small white pill.
A cruise ship docked in my blood
boards passengers who worship escape.
Present and past gods converse about the weather.
Should we make it snow?
They could use an intense rainstorm,
a deluge of implacable waves.

I'm not sure what to do about social media.
My algorithm considers me a democratic socialist.
I have a friend who lunched on Crayola crayons
during elementary school.
Access to wings would soothe my feet.
The conversation among trees fills me with wonder.
I flutter in a breeze of leaves.
Where's Rudy? replaces Where's Waldo?
Long ago persists in my mailbox.

So, what's up with you?
I hear you were accosted by aggressive media.
It's quite the rage like artificial intelligence.
I could use a cocktail of red roses,
the cessation of fierce regret.
Obstacle rhymes with popsicle.
My specialty: rhytidectomies for clichés.
I stay in my bowling lane.
Do you stay in yours?

Some nights, a cinema in my head
features strangers in love, a world
free of borders and battlefields.
Endangered species share and discuss their fate.
The audience demands popcorn and dialogue.
I roam the theater without a pocket flashlight,
drift with the electron clouds in my body
to a ethereal tune. When morning arrives,
I enter the sky.

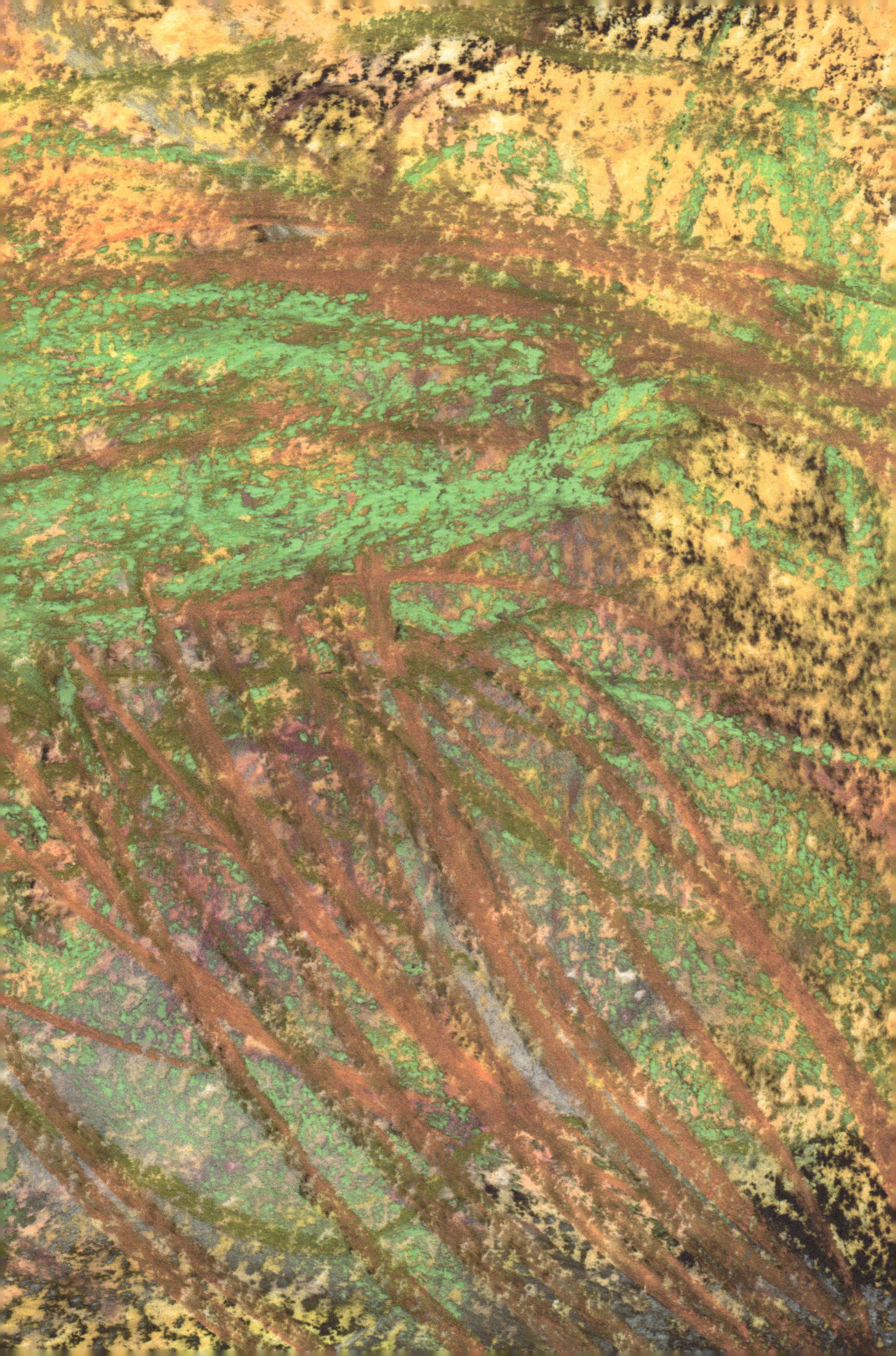

www.ingramcontent.com/pod-product-compliance
Lightning Source LLC
Chambersburg PA
CBHW041512120626
46551CB00018B/2401